Untold Stories

Untold Stories

The Latinx Leadership Experience in Higher Education

PETER RIOS

Foreword by Juan F. Martínez

WIPF & STOCK · Eugene, Oregon

UNTOLD STORIES
The Latinx Leadership Experience in Higher Education

Wipf & Stock
An Imprint of Wipf and Stock Publishers
199 W. 8th Ave., Suite 3
Eugene, OR 97401

www.wipfandstock.com

PAPERBACK ISBN: 978-1-6667-1697-9
HARDCOVER ISBN: 978-1-6667-1698-6
EBOOK ISBN: 978-1-6667-1699-3

11/11/21

Contents

Dedication

This book is dedicated to the Latinx community in the U.S. and abroad, but most importantly, to those Latina and Latino leaders who have paved the way for someone like me to have a place in higher education. A special thanks to the five executive Latinx leaders who gave their time to help with this research project by way of interview. Your stories are forever valued and will never be forgotten. And although I was not able to write the real names of Ruth, Yanisa, Marisol, Tomás, and Josue, I will always take refuge and inspiration from each of you, and what you have meant for our communities of faith.

To Dr. Laila E. Denoya and Dr. Roberto Denoya (RIP): You saw something special in me in high school when I did not believe in myself. You not only saw something in me and helped me to become the person I am today, but you have also served countless Latinx and other students, making it possible for so many to achieve their dreams. Thank you for always believing in me even when I did not. You helped me to graduate from high school and get into my first college, and you have journeyed with my wife and me through several life transitions. We can always count on you. You are one of the main reasons for such a research project on executive Latinx leaders. *Muchas gracias*!

Finally, but not least, to my beautiful and amazing wife, Dr. Ruby Gonzalez-Rios, you are such an inspiration: a true Latinx leader. Thank you for always being there for me and believing, encouraging, and pushing me to see more, and to pursue further graduate study. I am also so grateful for all the sacrifices you have made to allow me to pursue so many remarkable opportunities—even at the expense of your own career and calling. You agreed to go to Fuller Theological Seminary and to so many other things. I am very grateful. I love you, *amorcito*!

Foreword

I have served the Latinx church for most of my life and Christian higher education for the past two decades. My main areas of research and teaching have been in Latino Protestantism and identity, migration, and transnationalism. So, it was fitting when Peter Rios reached out to me in 2015 and asked if I would be his advisor for the PhD program in Intercultural Studies at Fuller Graduate Schools. When he arrived in the Fall of 2016, his research interests spanned the areas of diversity, the church and multicultural ministry, and possibly higher education. But like a good PhD mentor, I kept advising him to narrow down his research topic.

I suggested Peter start by reading about his own Puerto Rican heritage and the unique relationship of the U.S. with the Island. He did and became rather interested with issues surrounding the broader Latinx community, such as immigration and migration, socioeconomic status, educational access, racism, discrimination, and equity, but finally he found his niche—Latinx leadership in Christian higher education. At this intersection he would explore through his own life and professional experiences and that of others the realities of serving as a leader at predominantly White Evangelical institutions (PWEIs).

It has been well documented that present and future enrollment growth in colleges and universities are mostly from students of color with Latinx students currently leading in this development, especially in Christian higher education. As I have written elsewhere,[1] among Latinos, 64 percent attend evangelical schools, 20 percent mainline seminaries, and 16 percent Catholic institutions. As a result, what are colleges and universities doing to embrace this influx of diverse students and specifically the Latinx student body? Are PWEIs taking the initiative to create spaces of belonging? Are they being reactive or proactive with their diversity, equity, and inclusion efforts? How are these schools preparing their own leaders from within, or

1. See Martínez, *The Story of Latino Protestants in the United States*, 206.

recruiting Latinx and other minoritized leaders for this new reality? These are some of the questions that this book will explore.

As I have stated before, a new Latinx reality is emerging with Latinos[2] becoming the largest minoritized group in the U.S. And although a demographic growth is evident, this has not yet translated into political, social, economic, or religious influence of the same magnitude. However, Latinx are the fastest growing church and more religious than much of the U.S. population at large. About 20 percent of the Latinx population is Protestant, although there are countries in Latin America that have a higher percentage of Protestants.[3]

Latinx Protestants have a very diverse story and have often lived in an in-between space ethnically, religiously and socially—*Ni de aqui ni de alla*.[4] So, what happens when we (Latinx) serve at PWEIs that were not created with us in mind? The answer to this question is explored in depth in this book by interviewing a group of executive Latinx leaders who have served at the highest levels of the Council of Christian Colleges and Universities (CCCU). These are the *Untold Stories* you will encounter through the *testimonios* of Latinx leaders who have navigated the in-between spaces of PWEIs and their own Latinx identity and leadership service. They will share with you their over 128 years combined of higher education experiences in more than 20 CCCU schools, "the leading national voice of Christian higher education," and other nonreligious affiliated institutions of higher education.

It is clear to me, not only through this groundbreaking study, but also through my more than two decades of service in Christian higher education as an administrator, professor, and consultant, that change is not only needed—but indeed is now essential to the sustainability and the future existence of Christian colleges and universities. Without people of color, women, and other minoritized groups in senior leadership roles, Christian higher education runs the risk of becoming irrelevant. Peter Rios, in *Untold Stories*, lays out strategic solutions and a plausible future for such schools.

JUAN F. MARTÍNEZ, PH.D.
President, Centro Hispano de Estudios Teológicos (CHET)

2. I use the words Latino/Latinx/Latina interchangeably.

3. For a more detailed discussion of the statistics, see Martínez, *The Story of Latino Protestants in the United States*, 165-70.

4. "*Ni de aqui ni de alla*" is a common phrase shared in the Latino community that means "neither from here nor there," which points to the in-betweenness of Latinx in the US not feeling at home either in the US or back in Latin America.

Acknowledgments

This book would not be possible without the grace of Jesus. Thank you for being the rock of my life. I would also like to acknowledge *mi familia* close and far, my mother Andrea Diaz and father Pedro Rios (Pete Sr.); if it were not for you, I would not have been able to accomplish what I have fulfilled. To my grandmother Lourdes Mendez who raised me in the faith: *Gracias, mami*! A true apostle of the faith! And to all the church communities I have been a part of: you have shaped and formed me into the leader I am today. Throughout my time at Fuller, while living in Pasadena, CA, Ruby and I congregated at *la Iglesia del Pacto*, Eagle Rock, CA. We are forever indebted to you for all your love and hospitality–once Eagle Rock always Eagle Rock!

To both of my advisors while at Fuller, Juan F. Martínez and Douglas McConnell—thank you! I never would have enrolled at Fuller Theological Seminary if it were not to work with Dr. Martínez. Thank you for accepting me as a student and for giving me the opportunity to work with and learn from you, not only at Fuller, but at your house and our church. You have shown me what it is to be a true servant leader. Even after your health complications in 2019–2020, you came back to make sure you could see me through this important research. You exemplify what it is to be a Latinx leader in our community. I admire how you have labored so much to give *nuestro pueblo* (our people) a voice and place at the table. I am inspired by you to always give myself to the Latinx community, the broader society, and the church. To Dr. McConnell: I am convinced that I could not have completed this project if it were not for you. At one point, when Dr. Martínez could no longer provide direct leadership to me and this project due to life transitions, you took me on as a mentee and provided accountability, leadership, and coaching, not only for this work, but for life, vocation, and calling. I am inspired by you to always give myself to others in the academy.

To my editor, Elise Erikson Barret: I have read so many books and noticed how so many authors always thanked their editors. I could never appreciate that until now. Thank you for making this text better in so many ways. I hope we can do this again!

I am grateful to Fuller Theological Seminary School of Intercultural Studies, a place where persons can go and explore new ideas through innovation and creativity. To Dr. Amos Yong, CMR, and Johnny Ching: a special thank you for working with me and always being so accommodating. I am forever grateful to you for your leadership and service.

Finally, to Wipf and Stock Publishers, thank you for agreeing to work with me and to publish my work. Your staff are truly amazing!

List of Abbreviations

CCCU   Council of Christian Colleges and Universities

CHE   Christian Higher Education

CRT   Critical Race Theory

DEI   Diversity, Equity, and Inclusion

HSIs   Hispanic Serving Institutions

LatCrit   Latina/o Critical Theory

PWIs   Predominately White Institutions

Introduction

Reality is in the eye of the beholder.

—MIGUEL DE CERVANTES SAAVEDRA, DON QUIXOTE

This book stems from my own Christian higher education (CHE) experiences, along with practical service in higher education as an executive leader within the Council of Christian Colleges and Universities (CCCU) and affiliate institutions. The lack of professors and administrative leaders who could relate to my U.S. Latinx experience and context has been one of the main drivers for my desire to address diversity issues within CHE. While at my first graduate school, I did not have any professors of color, nor were there any administrative leaders of color. Although I did have two female professors, one was an adjunct with little influence. In my first doctoral studies program at Regent University, my experience was similar. And once again, I found the same situation during my second doctorate cohort phase at Fuller Theological Seminary, with my first four professors being White males who led the core curriculum.

This book addresses the diversity, equity, and inclusion (DEI) climate within CHE from a Latinx perspective, focusing on executive Latinx leaders and their stories and how leaders like this might assist in the diversification of the CHE enterprise. While serving in CHE as a faculty member and administrator, I have observed that there exists a disparity in DEI. White privilege and power are organizational and structural issues that seem to be addressed at the surface but not systemically or at CHEs root. After surveying the literature and considering my own personal experience alongside the experiences of other people of color in CHE, it is apparent that there is much work to be done to better serve a changing and ever-more-diverse student population. According to Pete Menjares in *Diversity Matters*, one of the fastest growing student bodies is Latinx; yet the Latinx representation in leadership at CCCU schools is limited. Menjares asserts, "This reality is registering on the minds of institutional leaders throughout the CCCU and has elevated the urgency of the 'diversity' conversation on many campuses; this conversation is currently being framed as a matter of 'institutional survival' across the council."[5] CHE will have to think strategically if it desires to serve these students with excellence.

While there exists much research in public higher education literature pertaining to people of color and women in leadership positions, as well as research focusing on Latinx in community colleges in general, there is a current void for Latinx leadership research in CHE. Research shows that Latinx are the fastest growing student population in higher education,[6] while in CHE students-of-color enrollments continue to grow while the White student population continues to decline.[7] However, Latinx administrators and other people of color (including women) at the executive level do not yet reflect these current student demographic trends.

Although there exists a growing body of literature on the lived experiences of Latinx leaders in public higher education, when I scanned the research there was very limited content on Latinx in CHE. Currently the number of executive Latinx leaders in the Council of Christian Colleges and Universities (CCCU) in particular are significantly underrepresented in senior leadership positions. To examine stories and counter-stories that may explain the dearth of Latinx leaders in CHE, I investigate through the lens of Critical Race Theory (CRT) and Latino/a Critical Race Theory (LatCrit) the experiences of Latinx leaders within the CCCU.

This book seeks to discover how the very limited numbers of Latinx leaders have attained their positions, how they have navigated predominantly (or dominantly) White evangelical institutions, and what has been the character of their overall experiences within the CCCU. The experiences of executive Latinx leaders in CHE and the CCCU are not well-documented; therefore, the aspiration of this text is to provide a foundation for future research. If CHE desires to survive the shifting of a majority-minority nation by 2044,[8] its leaders will have to address DEI issues that are pertinent to the CCCU. Hence, this book seeks to understand the experiences of executive Latinx leaders serving within the CCCU and higher education.

---

5. Longman, *Diversity Matters*, 12.

6. Chun and Evans, *Leading a Diversity Culture Shift*, 16–17.

7. Longman, *Diversity Matters*, 15–16.

8. Chun and Evans, *Leading a Diversity Culture Shift*, 16–17.

As a scholar conducting qualitative research, it is important for me to recognize my own bias, and to claim clearly that my own life is intertwined with this research on diversity in CHE. Although every scholar tries to handle their investigation with a level of professionalism and objectivity, all are subject to their humanity, whether they admit it or not. As Melissa Freeman reminds us, "research, like teaching, is a political act, in that, as researchers or instructors, we make conscious decisions about what to include, exclude, emphasize, and strive for."[9] For that reason, I begin this book by sharing my own critical and autoethnographical analysis of my intersectional experiences in CHE.[10]

9. Freeman, *Modes of Thinking*, 4.
10. DePouw, "Intersectionality and Critical Race Parenting," 55.

1

Why We Must Tell These Stories

For me, service in the US Special Forces in Central America was an epiphany. In combat zones I learned that the edifying story I had learned about my nation as a guardian and promoter of democracy was false. It took me many more years to explain exactly what was wrong with that history, and how a new and more accurate story might be told.[1]

IN THE BEGINNING

I was born in the Bronx, New York, and lived there for my first eight years of life. Along with two younger cousins, I was raised by my grandmother who had migrated to New York from Puerto Rico at the age of fifteen. My grandmother moved us from the Bronx to Dunkirk, NY, about a fifty-minute drive west of Buffalo. We were raised in a very strict religious Pentecostal home, where most things outside of church activity were scrutinized as potentially sinful.

We attended church services from 7 p.m. on Tuesdays, Thursdays, and Fridays. We also went to Sunday school in the morning, then returned after eating lunch at home for Sunday evening worship, usually from around 6 p.m. As I think back, I realize that it was considered essential to attend

---

1. Ortiz, African American and Latinx History, xi.

church services often since a consistent theology was that Christ was returning for the church soon.

Reflecting on these times, no one seemed concerned that children might have needed to get to bed at a decent time to be rested for school, or to have substantive time for studying or developing other gifts and talents that could contribute to society. I can remember that the most important things in life for my grandmother were Jesus, the church, and hard work. And although some of the nights were long and school was not necessarily a priority, having faith in Jesus was, and for that I am most grateful. My grandmother and her generation gave us what they had inherited: a fervent faith that they believed was more important than anything else. It was never a viable option for my grandmother to go to school. Looking back, I am sure she would have been successful if afforded the opportunity to study in an environment conducive to learning.

I moved with my mother around the age of twelve. I was very curious about what the world had to offer since the church always criticized it. This would be the beginning of a very unstructured life, the opposite of the very controlled and religious life I shared with my grandmother. The pursuit of education was a late phenomenon for me. I barely graduated high school due to a lack of personal motivation to learn, an unstable home and family, and limited mentors (to say the least). Growing up, I never received any encouragement from teachers or counselors about something positive that I could become, or any direction or conversation about college and vocation.

It was assumed that I would at best get into a trade school, or more likely get incarcerated or drop out of school. There may have been several reasons for this, one being the fact that I ended up having early encounters with the law and being expelled from school in the tenth grade. However, I never received any guidance while in middle school either. I also experienced prejudice in school growing up and witnessed how certain students from affluent backgrounds and from the majority culture always received favors for upward mobility. But God would provide an angel for me, someone who would believe in me and expose me to much more in life, primarily through the lens of education. Dr. Laila Denoya, the Director of the Upward Bound Program at SUNY Fredonia, convinced me to join Upward Bound in tenth grade. I would be a part of this program throughout the rest of my high school journey.

My grades in high school were not the best, so I enlisted in the U.S. Marine Corps. My first duty station was at Okinawa, Japan. This not only gave me global exposure but also allowed me to see my own ethnocentric ideologies and to become aware of American imperialism. I could not understand why the Okinawans did not want us there after all the U.S. had done for them, and why other cultures preferred to conduct themselves outside of what I deemed normal. As I got stationed in South Korea and California shortly thereafter, this all began to shape a new worldview within me, and I soon noticed the Puerto Rican youngster from NY being stretched and forced to change viewpoints that I once held as sacred, from culture to tradition, even my own denominational view of Christianity.

I had two tremendous personal encounters with Jesus Christ, one while serving in the Marines, and the other in New York a few years after my honorable discharge. These events transformed my life more profoundly than anything else, changing me from a worldly and religious person to someone who treasured an intimacy with Jesus through the Holy Spirit. I left my job and began to study in my denomination's biblical institute (in Spanish), simultaneously studying for an associate degree in pastoral studies at Houghton College's West Seneca Campus. This would be the start of my educational experience within the Council of Christian Colleges and Universities (CCCU). The program I was registered in closed due to the lack of enrollment before I could finish; therefore, I transferred to another religiously affiliated university online (Liberty University) to complete my B.S. in Religion.

I entered Northeastern Seminary (NES) at Roberts Wesleyan College right-after my undergraduate degree and noticed that most of my professors were male and White. The curriculum, while new and exciting in some respects, was also lacking diversity and voices from the Global South. It was difficult to translate this knowledge to my context. In other words, I had to contextualize information being taught to my own Latinx and multiethnic community. Around this time, I was also serving the broader church as a full-time evangelist, which connected me to many Latinx churches, customs, and ecclesial traditions. I noticed a common denominator among Pentecostal and Charismatic churches and their leadership: namely, the lack of formal theological or college education overall (although there were some exceptions). I ended up completing my M.A. in theological studies at NES and a doctoral degree in strategic leadership at Regent University, another CCCU school. An interesting detail is that my academic experience was similar at the doctoral level, with primarily White male professors and nondiverse coursework.

On May 6, 2016, my wife Ruby and I traveled to Regent University in Virginia Beach, VA, for my first doctoral commencement and commissioning service. I was ecstatic because I was going to be commissioned as a Christian leader to go and transform the world. The commissioning service for the School of Business and Leadership began, and they gave the microphone to Pat Robertson, Chancellor and CEO of Regent. He started well by

congratulating us and painting a future picture of success. However, shortly
thereafter he began to speak and exegete the Parable of the Talents found
in Matthew 25:14—30. If you have never read the Parable of the Talents, it
is a short story that Jesus shared about a person who was going on a long
journey:

> Again, it will be like a man going on a journey, who called his
> servants and entrusted his wealth to them. To one he gave five
> bags of gold, to another two bags, and to another one bag, each
> according to his ability. Then he went on his journey. The man
> who had received five bags of gold went at once and put his
> money to work and gained five bags more. So also, the one with
> two bags of gold gained two more. But the man who had re-
> ceived one bag went off, dug a hole in the ground and hid his
> master's money.
>
> After a long time the master of those servants returned and
> settled accounts with them. The man who had received five bags
> of gold brought the other five. "Master," he said, "you entrusted
> me with five bags of gold. See, I have gained five more." His
> master replied, "Well done, good and faithful servant! You have
> been faithful with a few things; I will put you in charge of many
> things. Come and share your master's happiness!" The man with
> two bags of gold also came. "Master," he said, "you entrusted
> me with two bags of gold; see, I have gained two more." His
> master replied, "Well done, good and faithful servant! You have
> been faithful with a few things; I will put you in charge of many
> things. Come and share your master's happiness!"
>
> Then the man who had received one bag of gold came.
> "Master," he said, "I knew that you are a hard man, harvesting
> where you have not sown and gathering where you have not
> scattered seed. So I was afraid and went out and hid your gold in
> the ground. See, here is what belongs to you." His master replied,
> "You wicked, lazy servant! So you knew that I harvest where
> I have not sown and gather where I have not scattered seed?
> Well then, you should have put my money on deposit with the
> bankers, so that when I returned, I would have received it back
> with interest. So, take the bag of gold from him and give it to the
> one who has ten bags. For whoever has will be given more, and
> they will have an abundance. Whoever does not have, even what
> they have will be taken from them. And throw that worthless
> servant outside, into the darkness, where there will be weeping
> and gnashing of teeth."

Pat Robertson began to interpret this pericope and in so doing began to ruin the night for many of the graduates. Pat took the liberty of tarnishing a wonderful moment of celebration and achievement to make comparisons between Republicans and Democrats in the United States. But this was just the beginning. He stated that "God took from the poor and gave to the rich" like the owner did in the Parable of Talents, taking one bag from the third servant who only had one and giving it to the person who had ten. Pat could not understand why "the Democrats were so upset with the Republicans" regarding how they leveraged their financial gains.

The most disappointing facet of all this for me and many others was the fact that the majority of Regent graduates were women and people of color. These graduates had paid a lot of money to enroll in this school and were not appreciated. Quite frankly, I felt used for their political conservative agenda. Unfortunately, I could not find a recording of this event and even contacted Regent University's manager of administration and events but was told that they did not record this commissioning (of course they didn't!). As I searched online, I found every other school's commissioning service at Regent for 2016 and thereafter. While I could not find the 2016 commissioning service, I did find Regent's School of Business and Leadership 2021 Commissioning, and this is an excerpt of what Pat communicated to the graduates:

> About 40 years ago the Lord spoke to me, and he said, "Build a school for my glory." I didn't realize in those days how important Regent University would be. I couldn't have foreseen a time in which the world was so torn apart with conflicting ideologies, a time when all the basic assumptions of our life would be challenged. A time when the United States of America, the greatest nation on earth, was in danger of becoming communists and socialists. I couldn't have dreamed that we would have a society in which perversion was being exalted and abortion was being made a constitutional right. . .I couldn't believe that little children in the elementary grades would be taught Critical Race Theory and that somehow America was a systemically racist society. I couldn't have believed that a major newspaper would publish something called the 1619 project which said America did not begin until the importation of slaves. Totally inaccurate, totally apart from our history, and we're trying to divorce our society from history.[2]

As you can see, not much changed with Pat from 2016 to 2021.

---

2. Regent University, Commissioning 2021.

If anything, Pat, and people like Pat, have doubled down in their ways. But this is only one experience among many that I can share from my experience within the enclave that is Christian higher education. Around this season of life, I felt compelled to address this situation of diversity and racism across Christian institutions and the evangelical church in the U.S., and decided to pursue another doctoral degree, this time at Fuller Theological Seminary at the PhD level. More than being compelled, I would say that I felt called to this work.

I originally went to Fuller to research the intricacies of culture and diversity issues in CHE. What led me to Fuller was my experience with racism in the Midwest while serving at a CCCU school. I experienced microaggressions and prejudice firsthand at this institution and local churches. While serving there, I was able to serve on numerous search committees for faculty and I witnessed how highly qualified candidates of color, sometimes more qualified than White candidates, were bypassed by the search committee or chair. At one point, the chair of a faculty search was prescreening applicants and sending us the ones that he believed were good "mission fits" for approval. I stated that this was not aligned with best practice but was silenced by other senior White faculty who seemed to appreciate what the chair was doing.

An African American colleague who also served at this institution once shared with me that he and his family were cautioned to stay out of a neighboring town. This specific town was still known as a "sundown town." We spoke together and counseled each other often. Since there were very few of us, it was important for us to seek each other out for prayer, and a space to vent about pressing issues. On another occasion, my colleague shared with me that an African American student's car was keyed (scratched up badly) with the words "get out of here nigger."

One final experience at this institution is worth noting, and that is the experience of my wife. My wife holds a PhD in biochemistry and is well-published, more than any other scientist on the staff or faculty of this institution at the time. We networked and tried everything possible to get her a position in this CCCU school, mainly since there was a lot of talk about how they wanted to diversify the staff and faculty, but there was always an excuse (including: no position open, no funding, overqualified, maybe next semester). There are very few women of color in science, particularly in the CCCU. One would think that if a university is intentional about recruiting and retaining staff and faculty of color, that they would be more strategic or even accommodating to couples. I witnessed over and over how the leadership would always make modifications for the majority culture in their hiring practices. By the end of my tenure, my wife had not even landed an adjunct teaching assignment. My African American colleague experienced the same treatment with his spouse. She was a very educated and talented professional who interviewed three times but never was considered for a position. At her last interview she was offered a position that she did not apply for; one that would have made her report to a White woman who had less education and experience. My colleague and family left disheartened less than a year later.

We eventually left the Midwest so I could study and research at Fuller, and although Pasadena was diverse, Fuller was not. My first four professors, the ones leading the core curriculum in our PhD cohort, were all White males. This was very discouraging for me. How could a graduate school providing leadership development for the majority evangelical world still be so White in the twenty-first century? At this point I was ready to rethink my academic study at Fuller; nonetheless, what kept me there was the encouragement of my colleagues, fellow students, and my previous advisor.

I left Fuller a year later because I accepted a position to serve as an executive leader in another CCCU school, also in the West. I assumed that since this school was a Hispanic Serving Institution (HSI), they surely would be serious about diversity, equity, and inclusion. This could not have been further from the truth. The same racism and discrimination were prevalent in this institution. I served on several search committees and cabinet interviews that seemed to ignore highly qualified candidates of color. In one instance, when searching for a dean of business, the search committee did not want a particular Latino in this position because, according to them, he was not qualified enough, although he held a PhD in a business field, was the chair of a business department, and had the business experience to qualify him. Subsequently, a White woman who had no education in business was chosen.

I experienced some very discouraging things while serving on the president's cabinet. Since I was the only Latino at the leadership table, I found myself always trying to advocate for Latinx students and other students of color. I experienced significant fatigue. Once, a White colleague asked if we could show fewer Hispanic students on video promotions. His perception was that the images of Hispanic students communicated less rigor and value. When I confronted him, he tried to circumvent the conversation by exclaiming that this was not his intention. We replaced three vice presidents while I was at this institution, and while there were many bright and highly gifted people of color who applied, none of them was offered the position. At one point I was told that "we needed our vice president of student affairs to be Hispanic" since most of our students were Latinx, and that the candidate needed to hold a doctorate. Although we had Latinas apply and other people of color with PhD/EdDs and much experience, a White man without a doctorate was chosen. The other two vice president positions were also filled by two White individuals.

I thought that my experiences were unique, like getting interviewed at a CCCU school in North Carolina and being asked by the president to identify my economic model, if I advocated for capitalism, and if I believed in White privilege. Of course, I responded, I believe in White privilege! Just like I believe in male privilege! I was also asked once in an interview with another CCCU president in Indiana if I thought I was being "called to their institution as some sort of prophet." But he framed it like this: "You don't believe that you are being called here to be some sort of prophet, do you?" In other words, "please do not think that you are going to come here and change us, because we do not want to change."

These are just some of the experiences that lead me to want to research and write about DEI matters in the CCCU from a Latinx perspective. My own experiences have fostered my curiosity to learn about other Latinx and their experiences in higher education. My hope and desire are that this contribution will help fellow colleagues in CHE to seek change and will encourage fellow Latinx leaders in their leadership roles. Developing cultural literacy and research knowledge, as well as awareness of the current diversity landscape of higher education, is important for their success.

RESEARCH METHODOLOGY

I use storytelling as a component of Critical Race Theory (CRT) to address diversity, equity, and inclusion (DEI) by interviewing executive Latinx leaders in CHE (see definition section). Storytelling helps the in-group or majority culture understand the narratives of those who have been marginalized and assigned certain stories that they themselves may not hold as truth.[3]

There are five recognizable tenets for CRT that provide the framework for this work, specifically challenging societal inequalities that help structures of oppression and privilege for some. These are (a) permanence of race, (b) color-blindness, (c) Whiteness as property, (d) interest convergence, and (e) counter-storytelling.[4] My focus utilizing CRT will be storytelling and counter-storytelling, an approach that gives voice to Latinx leaders in CHE. The leaders I interviewed all served the CCCU as deans or above (vice president, provosts, etc.), all hold PhDs, and with myself included, represent more

---

3. Delgado and Stefancic, Critical Race Theory, 71–72.
4. Delgado and Stefancic, Critical Race Theory, 8–11.

than 135 years of collective higher education experience across more than 20 CCCU institutions (and other institutions of higher education as well).

A full methods section is included in the Appendix, including a Christian rationale for using CRT and Latino/a Critical Race Theory for those who may have concerns with it. However, what I would say to those Christians now is that CRT is very much aligned with historic Christian values. For example, CRT provides the platform for the narratives of marginalized people to get presented. This, in my opinion, mirrors the Christian faith practice of using testimony to speak about experiences with God in and out of the church. Likewise, the primitive church used oral tradition to teach early believers about Jesus since the Bible was not yet written. If we have issues with people sharing their experiences and stories, then we might just as well have true trepidation about the book of Luke (and other books in the Christian scriptures) since they also tell a story and relate experiences that they heard from others:

> Many have undertaken to draw up an account of the things that have been fulfilled among us, just as they were handed down to us by those who from the first were eyewitnesses and servants of the word. With this in mind, since I myself have carefully investigated everything from the beginning, I too decided to write an orderly account for you, most excellent Theophilus, so that you may know the certainty of the things you have been taught (Luke 1:14, NIV)

This book provides one piece of the puzzle needed to move towards a more inclusive and equitable future for Christian higher education (CHE). CHE leadership is mainly White and male, but there is potential to create spaces for others to serve and lead. There is a major gap in the literature when dealing with administrators of color, especially with Latinas.[5] My research is an attempt to fill this void by giving voice to those who have historically been suppressed by the dominant narrative.

My hopes and aspirations are to contribute significantly to the literature dealing with Latinx leaders in CHE, to provide the resources necessary to enable other Latinx to grow and mature, and to make further contributions to diversity and intercultural relations in the CCCU. I am concerned that if the CCCU does not become more aggressive with its diversity efforts, the ministry of CHE will be significantly hindered. I desire for the CCCU not only to survive, but to thrive and flourish in the twenty-first century.

---

5. Please see the following works for evidence of this gap: Núñez et al., "Latinos in Higher Education"; Moffit, "Narrative Study"; Núñez et al, Hispanic-Serving Institutions; and Smith, Diversity's Promise.

Latinx contributions to leadership involve three crucial particularities that enrich and shape the mission of CHE. First, the importance of access and cultural relevance as represented by the Latinx growth in the USA means that cultural representation in leadership is needed urgently. Second, the mission of CHE is crucial for the *Missio Dei* overall and its definition as viewed by Critical Race Theory, having to do with relationality. Latinx are community-oriented people.[6] The Latinx presence in academic administration will help shape the institutional ethos. Thirdly, the diversity of administrators has the potential to create synergy for change at a time when change is characterizing the educational enterprise.

Latinx are the fastest-growing population in the U.S. and tend to be very religious; hence, Latinx will play a key role in the CCCU's future. The presence of Latinx leaders in academic administration will help as a catalyst, along with other diversity representatives, in contextualizing CHE for contemporary needs. If the primary mission of CHE is to serve the church by equipping her for her calling to serve the world, then keeping well-informed of demographic shifts and educational trends will be vital for building a diverse institutional capacity, and in fact, will be vital for CHE's very existence.[7]

6. Malavé and Giordani, Latino Stats, 57.

7. Kemeny, Faith, Freedom, and Higher Education, 90–91.

2

Positioning Latinx Leadership in Higher Education

One of the defining labels I have for myself, and perhaps we can do this better than other cultures . . . The word is *chameleon*. My ability to walk into a setting and not lose who I am. Not lose any of me. From my identity to manifestation of behavior being shifted and adjusted. Not to sell out or to change who you are, but to really manifest a sense of efficacy, efficiency, and competence that gives you the opportunity to actually move forward. So how can I get a team of people who have never had a person of color, specifically a Latino, to supervise them to be influenced, led and motivated and bring vision and all these things . . . I have to be able to connect to language, context, and understand my audience . . . I have to understand the language that they speak. So, all of those things are a part of that. Therefore, for me, the word that comes to mind in terms of cross-cultural, intercultural training for Latinos in particular, is your capacity to become a chameleon. You don't lose who you are, you are everything of who you are, and that shows in many ways. Then you are able to make the adjustments necessary in order to influence.[1]

Leadership is a very complex topic with many different definitions, and the conception of leadership has evolved significantly over time. For example,

1. Tomás.

from 1900–1929, leadership primarily was expressed through control, centralization of power, and, of course, dominance.[2] During the 1930s—1940s, personality traits were the main leadership emphasis, while in the 1940s, groups and the concept of coercion became a primary focus. Furthermore, in the 1950s—1960s, although there was no major world crisis, there was a continuance of emphasis on groups and shared goals, and specifically the leader as influencer.[3] The 1970s saw an emerging focus on organizational behavior and leadership models, while the 1980s exploded with scholarly work on influence, traits, and the transformation of organizations and followers.[4]

DEFINING LEADERSHIP

Leadership theory has evolved, much like the people who exercise it. Prior to the twentieth century, people associated leadership with elevated positions. Leadership studies began with the assumption that "leaders were born with special gifts that made them different from ordinary mortals."[5] The twenty-first century introduced the major debate regarding whether leadership and management were any different in process; while types of leadership (authentic, spiritual, servant, and adaptive) took precedence in scholarship.[6] Throughout all these years of dissention among scholars and practitioners of leadership, one thing is certain: there is no common definition of leadership. For my purposes, G. Peter Northouse is helpful: leadership is the "process whereby an individual influences a group of individuals to achieve a common goal."[7]

Leadership, then, involves the exercise of influence from leader to follower and from follower to leader; it occurs in groups, and leaders mostly have their attention on the goals that they desire to fulfill. "Two common forms of leadership are assigned and emergent. Assigned leadership is based on a formal title or position in an organization. Emergent leadership results from what one does and how one acquires support from followers. Leadership, as a process, applies to individuals in both assigned

---

2. Northouse, Leadership, 2.
3. Yukl, Leadership in Organizations, 7.
4. Northouse, Leadership, 4.
5. Bolman and Deal, Reframing Organizations, 344.
6. Northouse, Leadership, 5.
7. Northouse, Leadership, 6.

roles and emergent roles."[8] Furthermore, leaders are born and nurtured through a lifelong journey and process.[9]

The literature suggests that leaders will need to be strategic in times of change. "Individuals and teams enact strategic leadership when they think, act, and influence in ways that promote the sustainable competitive advantage of the organization."[10] The main mission of strategic leaders is the success of their organization. In other words, they are concerned with the efficiency and effectiveness of their organization, as well as their followers. They keep long-term goals in mind and always keep abreast of short-term objectives.[11] Excellent leaders enable their organizations to be learning organizations.

Leaders are people that others seem to admire. Followers seek leaders to create solutions for them and their organization, and leaders are also sought after to manage change and transformation within organizations. Strategic leadership is more about process than it is about position.[12] It involves a team effort of individuals and organizations accepting their own load of responsibility for the vision, thinking, and execution of strategic plans. Good managers bring a great deal of consistency and order to an organization, while leaders do well with facilitating change. Therefore, change is what drives leaders to be visionaries and innovators. While managers usually excel with "business as usual" scenarios, leaders feed off uncertainty, change, and the next exciting venture. Nevertheless, leadership "is a complex phenomenon involving the leader, the followers, and the situation."[13]

Leaders differentiate most from managers in that they live and lead from the future. As the all-time great Wayne Gretzky once said, "a good hockey player plays where the puck is. A great hockey player plays where the puck is going to be."[14] In other words, great leaders anticipate where things are going because they study their context well. They do not aspire to get everything right about the future,[15] since they are aware that no one can predict the future with accuracy. However, "foresight leaders" claim two

8. Northouse, Leadership, 16.

9. McConnell, Cultural Insights, 34. Cognitive studies tell us that people are interdependent of culture and human nature. In essence then, leaders are both born and made.

10. Hughes and Beatty, Becoming a Strategic Leader, 9.

11. Hughes and Beatty, Becoming a Strategic Leader, 12.

12. Hughes and Beatty, Becoming a Strategic Leader, 5.

13. Hughes et al, Leadership: Enhancing the Lessons, 5.

14. As cited in De Jong, Anticipate, 83.

15. Gordon, Future Savvy, 23.

certainties about the future; you either align yourself and your organization with the future, or you create the future.[16]

It is important to state here that most leadership theories extant in today's literature come from a Eurocentric framework, making "leadership" a contested term with a male, Eurocentric imaging. This book attempts to understand leadership from a Latinx perspective that will add value to the current literature more broadly, and the Latinx community specifically.

POSITIONING CHRISTIAN LEADERSHIP

Christian leaders have a different set of standards and benchmarks from their secular colleagues. Christian leaders draw from "biblical insights and secular wisdom" as an imperative.[17] Jesus can be considered one of the greatest leaders of all time since diverse manifestations of his organization are still alive and well after two millennia. Thus, a closer look at how Jesus led is essential. Jesus was counter-cultural compared to the contemporary Greco-Roman society. Jesus made it his mission to demonstrate to the disciples what true leadership was, and how this leadership should be lived out. Jesus declared on one occasion:

> You know that the rulers of the Gentiles lord it over them, and their high officials exercise authority over them. Not so with you. Instead, whoever wants to become great among you must be your servant, and whoever wants to be first must be your slave— just as the Son of Man did not come to be served, but to serve, and to give his life as a ransom for many (Matthew 20:25–28, NIV).

Jesus situates what good leadership looks like in this passage from Matthew 20. Jesus stated that he did not come to be served but to serve. Put another way, if Jesus' followers desire to be good leaders, they will have to be servant leaders. Robert Greenleaf coined the term *servant leadership* in the 1970s,[18] but Jesus exhibited this behavior in the first century. Greenleaf defined servant leadership as follows: " . . . it begins with the natural feeling that one wants to serve, to serve first. This conscious choice brings one to aspire to lead." He goes on to declare:

> The difference manifests itself in the care taken by the servant first to make sure that other people's highest priority needs are being served. The best test, and difficult to administer, is:

16. Gordon, Future Savvy, 13.
17. Gibbs, Leadership Next, 21.
18. Northouse, Leadership, 225.

do those served grow as persons; do they, while being served, become healthier, wiser, freer, more autonomous, more likely themselves to become servants? And, what is the effect on the least privileged in society; will they benefit, or, at least, will they not be further deprived?[19]

Northouse lists what Spears identified as ten characteristics of servant leaders: listening, empathy, healing, awareness, persuasion, conceptualization, foresight, stewardship, commitment to the growth of people, and building community.[20] Jesus demonstrated all these qualities in his earthly ministry.

Christian leadership should be unique and different from secular leadership. J. Robert Clinton defines leadership "as a dynamic process in which a man or a woman with God given capacity influences a specific group of people towards his purposes for the group."[21] Christian leaders influence but do not dominate or "lord" over others. It is interesting to note that in the book of Genesis God commanded humans to govern over the earth and over every living creature (as good stewards), but never over another human (Gen 1:28). Therefore, as Jesus was counter-cultural in his time, so will contemporary Christian leaders be counter-cultural in their leadership. These Christian leaders ought to also be visionaries, seeing the invisible and making it visible for their followers. As George Barna declares, "vision for ministry is a clear mental image of a preferable future imparted by God to His chosen servants and is based upon an accurate understanding of God, self and circumstances."[22] And as the Scriptures remind us, where there is [no] vision the people of God will perish (Prov 29:18, KJV). Lastly, Christian leaders are lifelong learners who are "students of culture so [they can] lead wisely in an era of globalization."[23]

A FRAMEWORK FOR LATINX LEADERSHIP

Latinas in the U.S. have traditionally told their stories from the margins.[24] This may explain why "Latino leadership in higher education has escaped serious study."[25] Nevertheless, their stories are being told. For many, Latinx

19. Greenleaf, Servant as Leader, 15.

20. Northouse, Leadership, 227.

21. Clinton, Making of a Leader, 14.

22. Barna, Power of Vision, 26.

23. McConnell, Cultural Insights, xiii.

24. Martínez, Story of Latino Protestants, 186.

25. León and Martinez, Latino College Presidents, 3.

leadership starts in their community and is for their community.[26] Like other leaders of color, Latinx desire to create social change and impact for the betterment of the people. They also lead from a relational culture.[27] Juana Bordas explains this concept further:

> No matter how important a leader becomes, she or he must be willing to do the hard work needed for community progress. Leaders are expected to roll up their sleeves, stuff envelopes, clean up, cook, and serve food. Any type of elitism or projection that one is above certain tasks will destroy a leader's credibility. Leaders also earn respect by being accessible and generously giving of their resources and talents. They work hand in hand with people, leading not just by words but also by actions.[28]

Latinx leadership is as diverse as leaders' backgrounds and families, including particularities such as immigration and generational status; code switching and leadership styles; contextual specifics; and their diverse community role models. Latinx lead in churches, educational institutions, their communities, jobs, and careers. Bordas, in one of the first books on Latinx leadership, asserts that Latino leadership ". . .is one of coalition building, bringing people together, working across sectors, and embracing a consciousness of partnership. Latino leaders leverage the power of inclusion."[29]

It was during the Civil Rights era that Latinx leadership took center stage with César Chávez and Dolores Huerta founding the United Farm Workers of America. This group wanted to address the disparities of low wages and social-political issues that Latinas were facing in the Central Valley of California. Chávez has been referred to as the equivalent of what Rev. Dr. Martin Luther King symbolized for African Americans; and has been described as the world's most famous Latino.[30]

As evidenced by the Civil Rights movement, Latinx leaders are usually connected with their community and understand the complexity of culture, are bilingual and bicultural, and can relate with broader constituencies.[31] They also have a good spiritual awareness and connect their leadership with a higher calling.[32] Likewise, Bordas outlined ten Latino leadership principles:

26. Davis, "Latino Leadership Development," 230; Bordas, "Salsa, Soul, and Spirit, 71.
27. Klenke, Women in Leadership, 217.
28. Bordas, Salsa, Soul, and Spirit, 89.
29. Bordas, Power of Latino Leadership Culture, 13.
30. Romero, Brown Church, 120.
31. Villarruel, "Framework for Latino Nursing Leadership," 350.
32. Romero, Brown Church, 120–141; Lopez, "Pa'Lante!, Toward the Presidency,"

1. Personalismo—the character of the leader

2. Conciencia—knowing oneself and personal awareness

3. Destino—personal and collective

4. La Cultura—culturally based leadership

5. De Colores—inclusiveness and diversity

6. Juntos—collective community stewardship

7. Adelante—global vision and immigrant spirit

8. Si Se Puede—social activism and coalition leadership

9. Gozar la Vida—leadership that celebrates life

10. Fe y Esperanza—sustained by faith and hope[33]

It is important to note that all Latinas cannot be put into one box. Latinx are not a race but an ethnic group that is comprised of many hybrids and beautiful mixes of people. This section is added to enhance value to leadership literature specifically focusing on the Latinx community. Later in this book, we will explore the responses of interviewees who were asked about their leadership experience and what type of approach they have used in their professional journey, to shed light on future explorations of executive Latinx leadership.

CONTEXTUAL LEADERSHIP

In this section, it seemed appropriate to expand on a leadership theory that combined the notions of adaptability and contextual theology in an application to understanding leadership service. This is known as contextual leadership. But first we will examine missiology and contextualization as it applies to Latinx leadership.

I define missiology in the contemporary era in this way: "partnering with the Trinitarian God throughout the world for the *Missio Dei*." One area of missiology that has done well at grasping this idea has been the academic study and practice of contextualization. Contextual theology can be defined as a theological approach in which one takes into account: the spirit and message of the gospel; the tradition of the Christian people; the culture in which one is theologizing; and social change in that culture, whether

230–233.

33. Bordas, Power of Latino Leadership Culture, 26–139. It is interesting to note that the Latinx interviewed for this book confirm many of these assertions by Bordas related to Latinx leadership.

brought about by Western technological process or grass-roots struggle for equality, justice, and liberation.[34]

Contextualization is a global phenomenon that needs to be addressed by CHE, especially if she wants her message of Jesus to be fresh and relevant. As Bevans declares, "the contextualization of theology—the attempt to understand Christian faith in terms of a particular context—is really a theological imperative. As we understand theology today, contextualization is part of the very nature of theology itself."[35]

When considering a contextual missiology, one is concerned with the practice of faith, while simultaneously engaging cultural values, traditions, and contexts.[36] Although contextualization initiated in ecumenical circles,[37] evangelicals and conservatives have utilized the study and practice because of its value. According to Moreau, "contextualization captures the tension of Christians having biblical revelation that is universally true and applicable while living in a world of societies that are widely diverse in their religious identities." Moreau further argues that the message of the gospel through the church is expressed by the Scriptures while cultivated by the local culture.[38]

The contextualization dialogue that has historically circulated in the West, its theological institutions, and the church, primarily has been related to anthropological or social-cultural analysis. On the other hand, Matthew Kutz developed a contextual intelligence model, in which contextualization means "to be aware of the different variables that are being brought to a situation and then accurately discern between alternate courses of action to select the best action and then execute it."[39] Kutz further writes that leaders will need to embrace 3D Thinking (three-dimensional thinking) through hindsight, insight and foresight, which will give them a more accurate understanding of what was, what is, and what can be. And finally, contextual intelligence involves leveraging learning, reframing experience, and embracing complexity, which means diagnosing one's surroundings to better assess the context that would influence the behavior of both leaders and those they seek to lead.[40]

The landscape in which people lead today has become far more versatile, with factors like globalization having ubiquitous impact and presenting

34. Bevans, Models of Contextual Theology, 1.
35. Bevans, Models of Contextual Theology, 1.
36. Moreau, Contextualization in World Missions, 18.
37. Moreau, Contextualization in World Missions, 34.
38. Moreau, Contextualization in World Missions, 35.
39. Kutz, Contextual Intelligence, 16.
40. Kutz, Contextual Intelligence, 10.

unforeseen opportunities and challenges. Contextual intelligence gives leaders a model via which they can respond to the ever-changing environment. Kutz identifies twelve behaviors that successful leaders practice:

- Change agent—demonstrates the courage to raise difficult and challenging questions that others may perceive as a threat to the status quo.
- Communitarian—demonstrates involvement in community and civic responsibilities. Embraces civic obligations wholeheartedly. Sees connections between civic responsibility and workplace mission.
- Consensus builder—demonstrates collaboration by convincing others of the value in a needed idea or valid point of view.
- Critical thinker—connects disconnected ideas and experiences.
- Diagnoses context—interprets and responds to shifts or changes in one's surroundings, and can identify what contributed toward that shift.
- Constructive use of influence—demonstrates the effective use of different types of power in developing an image.
- Embraces diverse ideas—aligns diverse ideas by creating and facilitating opportunities for people with diverse backgrounds or experiences to interact in a non-discriminatory manner.
- Future minded—sees beyond contradictions (or obstacles) to a future others cannot yet see. Articulates that future to others clearly and succinctly.
- Influencer—demonstrates interpersonal skill by non-coercively affecting the actions and decisions of others.
- Intentional leadership—demonstrates awareness of and is proactive concerning their strengths and weakness.
- Mission minded—recognizes how they (their performance, attitude, and actions) influence what others perceive to be true about themselves and people or organizations they represent.
- Multicultural leadership—builds rapport with ethically and culturally diverse individuals.[41]

Contextual intelligence therefore provides leaders with the savviness needed to lead from the future, while remaining present and respecting the past. Contextual leaders are those who exegete their context for the mission of

---

41. Kutz, Contextual Intelligence, 13.

God in their lives and organizations and use every tool and skillset available to accomplish their mission and vision.[42]

Lastly, when it comes to the context of higher education, another leadership strategy has emerged—strategic diversity leadership. Damon A. Williams asserts that the external environment has evolved, and diversity efforts can no longer be left to happenstance.[43] Said differently, institutions of higher learning need to be intentional about their strategies and organizational leadership to diversify their colleges and universities. Strategic diversity leadership consists of five principles:

- Redefine issues of diversity, equity, and inclusion as fundamental to the organizational bottom line of mission fulfillment and institutional excellence.
- Focus on creating systems that enable all students, faculty, and staff to thrive and achieve their maximum potential.
- Achieve a more robust and integrated diversity approach that builds on prior diversity models and operates in a strategic, evidence-based, and data-driven manner, where accountability is paramount.
- Focus diversity-related efforts to intentionally transform the institutional culture, not just to make tactical moves that lead to poorly integrated efforts and symbolic implementation alone.
- Lead with a high degree of cultural intelligence and awareness of different identities and their significance in higher education (Williams, 14).

Strategic diversity leadership is concerned with the diversification of an organization. These leaders attend to the internal and external factors that prohibit an institution to move more towards a justice driven outcome. These leaders are working to create organizations where all humans can flourish, and in which access, diversity, equity and inclusion are priorities.

ORGANIZATIONAL CULTURE AND LEADERSHIP

Up to this point I have defined leadership theory in general and positioned faith-based leadership specifically for this book. Additionally, contextual leadership and contextual intelligence also have been presented. In this next

---

42. An analysis of interviews in this book supports a nuanced application of an integrated theoretical framework representing the combined works of J. Bordas, M. Kutz, and D. Williams.

43. Williams, Strategic Diversity Leadership, 13.

section, I present organizational culture and leadership to provide a culminating strategic overview of how this all works together.

Organizational culture, although very complex, can be defined simply as the way things are done in a specific organization.[44] But for this book, I use Edgar H. Schein's definition:

> The culture of a group can be defined as the accumulated shared learning of that group as it solves its problems of external adaptation and internal integration; which has worked well enough to be considered valid and, therefore, to be taught to new members as the correct way to perceive, think, feel, and behave in relation to those problems. This accumulated learning is a pattern or system of beliefs, values, and behavioral norms that come to be taken for granted as basic assumptions and eventually drop out of awareness.[45]

The system that is created out of patterns of beliefs is what keeps an organization in rhythm and what holds all the moving parts together. As stated above, once they have been embraced as normative for the organization, these "values and behavior norms" are what create and uphold a culture.

Organizational culture is created, shared and learned through experiences of its members and the implementation of its leaders through a process of socialization and acculturation.[46] This occurs within macro and micro cultures. Macro cultures can refer to "nations, ethnic groups, religions" and occupations and large organizations,[47] and microcultures (also known as subcultures) are those smaller units, groups or teams that make up the larger one.[48] For example, a global organization like IBM can have a microculture within the organization created by its mission and vision, but the way that is manifested throughout the world in different parts of the company may vary because of its subcultures. Leaders are then entrusted with the work of embodying these macro and micro cultures for the organization to have a predetermined measure of success.

Leaders and other members of an organization also must navigate other frameworks beyond the macro and micro cultures. Lee G. Bolman and Terrence E. Deal speak of four frames that every organizational leader must navigate. A frame is "a coherent set of ideas or beliefs forming a prism or lens that enables you to see and understand more clearly what goes on

44. Schein, Organizational Culture and Leadership, 5.
45. Schein Organizational Culture and Leadership, 6.
46. Schein, Organizational Culture and Leadership, 15.
47. Schein, Organizational Culture and Leadership, 13.
48. Schein, Organizational Culture and Leadership, xiii.

from day to day."[49] These organizational frames are: (1) the structural frame, which deals with design, (2) the human resource frame, which "centers on what organizations and people do to and for one another," (3) the political frame, which describes how decisions are made and resources are allocated, and (4) the symbolic frame, which includes symbols that give meaning to humans within their given organization.[50] All four frames are important in determining how an organization is led and operated.

Leaders in the twenty-first century will need to understand organizational culture as well as all the social constructs that have internal and external influence over the organization and its systems. As Branson and Martínez assert, "leadership . . . needs to be studied as an element of our context—the societal context—as well as cultural and local contexts."[51] In other words, leaders do not operate or serve in silos or vacuums but within a unit, group of people, or organization that is connected to other people in different ways. As Schein states, "leadership and culture formation are two sides of the same coin."[52]

Culture is fluid and never stagnant, ever changing and evolving; this is true whether in ethnic groups, religions, or organizations. And culture is the force that guides people and leaders on decision-making and direction for organizations. Edna Chun and Alvin Evans describe this idea in the following way: "the construct of culture has been described in metaphorical terms as a tapestry or a web. As an amorphous yet influential force, it guides the behaviors of individuals and groups and provides a frame of reference for interpretation of events."[53] Organizational culture is therefore a driving force in an organization that cannot be ignored, since leaders and other members are assessed as good or bad fits for the organization.[54]

Finally, cognitive studies and the elements of culture and human nature have been studied to help illuminate what makes human beings behave the way they do.[55] As Heibert asserts, "trying to understand people as humans always involves the process of interpreting their beliefs, feelings, and values from their own points of view."[56] Said differently, studying behaviors

49. Bolman and Deal, Reframing Organizations, 41.

50. Bolman and Deal, Reframing Organizations, 183–184.

51. Branson and Martínez, Churches, Cultures, and Leadership, 210.

52. Schein, Organizational Culture and Leadership, xiv.

53. Chun and Evans, Leading a Diversity Culture Shift, 104.

54. The concept of organizational fit is more fully developed and explored later in this book, as Latinx explain the concept of "mission fit" within the CCCU.

55. Heibert, Gospel in Human Contexts, 105.

56. Heibert, Gospel in Human Contexts, 105.

alone is not enough to understand people. Comprehension requires grappling with how persons reason and the process by which their minds come to certain conclusions.

Cognitive studies basically address what it means to be human.[57] And since our humanness is played out within the organizations we serve, their cultures and their internal and external contexts, how people process information, values, and actions is invaluable to organizational culture and leadership.[58] How people think about themselves and others, their families, and the surrounding communities, also affects other people and their organizations. Therefore, creating a diverse organization of people is important for learning and human flourishing, because it has the potential to provide a new set of experiences along with a platform for creativity and innovation.

LATINX STATISTICS

Latinas are the fastest growing population group in the U.S.,[59] and most forecast that by 2050 the U.S. will be a majority-minority country.[60] Other forecasts predict that Latinos will outnumber most ethnic groups in the U.S. by 2043,[61] although some find evidence that this has already occurred. Yet despite this seismic population shift, Latinos are still the least served in our society when it comes to formal higher education.

The Latinx population in the U.S. reached 56.6 million by July 2015,[62] with Latinas presently comprising 18.1% of the total population).[63] According to the Hispanic Association of Colleges and Universities (HACU), there were 3.29 million Latinos enrolled in nonprofit institutions of higher education in 2016. Over the past decade, Latina high school dropout rates have declined while college enrollment has increased.[64]

In January 2018, the CCCU published *The Case for Christian Higher Education*. The total CCCU global student enrollment is 520,000 while 445,000 in U.S. institutions. According to the CCCU, "since the turn of the century, the racial and ethnic composition of CCCU's campuses have

---

57. McConnell, Cultural Insights, 26.
58. McConnell, Cultural Insights, 31.
59. Malavé and Giordani, Latino Stats, 1.
60. Bastedo et al, American Higher Education, 376.
61. Batista et al, Latinx/a/os in Higher Education, xviii.
62. Batista et al, Latinx/a/os in Higher Education, xviii.
63. United States Census Bureau, "Quick Facts."
64. Krogstad, Jens Manuel, "5 Facts about Latinos."

become markedly more diverse."[65] Thirty-three percent of CCCU students are first generation, compared to 30.2% at four-year private institutions in the U.S. In other words, the percentage of first-generation and diverse students seems to be growing faster at Christian institutions.

The CCCU has seen growth in its Latinx student body. In 1999, the Latinx student body made up 3.7 percent of total enrollment at CCCU schools, while by 2015 it had grown to 9.6 percent.[66] Furthermore, in 2017–18, the total Latinx student body at CCCU schools was 10.62 percent, while the Latinx faculty was a far lower 3.59 percent and the Latinx administration 4.07 percent.[67] This data suggests that the Latinx community continues to grow in college interest and enrollment and will play a significant role in future academic success and financial stability for institutions in the CCCU. According to the U.S. Census Bureau, degree attainment in the U.S. by population group over twenty-five years old with a bachelors or above is: (1) Latinx 18.8 percent, (2) Black 26.1 percent, (3) White 40.1 percent, and (4) Asian 52.4 percent.[68] One concern that will need to be addressed is retention and graduation of these diverse students.

Adjusting to the cultural shift of Latinx within the U.S. is an essential priority for Christian higher education because of the specific nature of its identity and calling. Beyond this, however, the cultural shift that has occurred and will continue in the U.S. should concern everyone. The Lumina Foundation's President Jamie P. Merisotis stated, "for the nation to attain, not just economic security, but social justice and cohesion, college success must expand dramatically."[69]

The Latino community is much younger than the general national and state populations; in 2010, the average age of United States Latinas was twenty-seven, whereas the average age of Whites and non-Latinos was forty.[70] According to the U.S. Census Income and Poverty Report (2014), the average median income for populations in the U.S. were as follows: Latino$39,572, White$54,487, Black$33,805, and Asian$69,633. Latinos are not only the youngest group in the U.S., but are the fastest-growing population, the least educated and among the poorest. Yet, they also comprise

65. Council of Christian Colleges and Universities, "Case for Christian Higher Education."

66. Council of Christian Colleges and Universities, "Case for Christian Higher Education."

67. Council of Christian Colleges and Universities, Diversity Matters.

68. United States Census Bureau, "New Educational Attainment Data."

69. Lumina Foundation, "A Stronger Nation," 1.

70. Santiago and Callan, "Ensuring America's Future."

the fastest-growing church population.[71] Christian higher education has a missional opportunity to make a difference with this generation of Latinas.

These numbers are somewhat frightening, especially when the number of Latinx is projected to surpass other populations in the U.S. by 2030, factoring in that Latinos represent the lowest percentage of program enrollment and degree completion. As the Lumina Foundation asserts, "gaps in attainment are increasingly worrisome because postsecondary credentials are the gateway to full participation in society."[72] Today, this "full participation" can refer to voting, power dynamics in society, and organizational leadership.

EXECUTIVE LATINX LEADERS IN CHRISTIAN HIGHER EDUCATION

Latinx leadership scholarship in higher education has been somewhat limited,[73] and executive Latinx leadership explorations are difficult, simply put. To add complexity to the issue, if one divides specific identities (community college versus four-year institutions, for example, or religious versus nonreligious contexts), research becomes even more layered and complicated.

Latinx are the least represented in higher education within the ranks of faculty, staff, and administration. Latinas did not enter the higher education conversation until the Civil Rights Movement of the 1960s.[74] "Latinos comprise only 4.2 percent of the faculty in higher education, while White Americans comprise 79.0 percent. And in the administrative/managerial ranks, Latinos comprise 5.1 percent while White Americans [represent] 80.8 percent."[75] These statistics imply what we may have already intuited: there exists a diversity issue within the ranks of leadership in higher education.

Michael Moffit asserts, "research has indicated that the number of administrators of color who work at non-religious institutions is twice the number as those who work at religiously-affiliated higher education institutions."[76] Research on executive Latinx leaders is in its infancy stage within the CCCU. In 2014, there were 26,106 full and part-time faculty in the CCCU, with the Latinx representation at 2.48 percent. The CCCU

71. Barna Group, Hispanic America, 46.
72. Lumina Foundation, "A Stronger Nation," 3.
73. Savala, "The Experiences of Latina/o Executives," 150.
74. León and Martinez, Latino College Presidents, 3.
75. León and Martinez, Latino College Presidents, 2.
76. Moffit, "Executive Administrators of Color," 127.

employs 72,000 faculty and staff.[77] Data on Latinx administrators within the CCCU is currently nonexistent, making this research project essential. On this subject, Menjares declares:

> Relative to race and ethnicity, colleges and universities across the council vary in the proportion of diversity for students, staff, faculty, administrators, and trustees. Additionally, institutions are at different levels of understanding and stages of engagement with the principles of diversity, inclusion, and racial reconciliation. A growing number of our colleges and universities have significant numerical diversity in addition to robust infrastructure to support curricular and cocurricular programs, initiatives, and personnel. Other institutions are beginning to see increasing diversity among their students and for the first time are entering the conversation of what it means to be diverse and inclusive.[78]

Research demonstrates that the population of Latinas is growing in society and in higher education enrollment. Where Latinx have not seen exponential growth is in the executive leadership of colleges and universities, especially Christian institutions. The slow growth of Latinx leaders seems to be counter indicative to enrollment goals for CCCU schools since Latinx faculty and administration play an important role in Latinx student success, because they understand broadly their culture, language, and narratives.[79]

The question remains: why are we not seeing more people of color in executive leadership positions in higher education? More specifically, why the dearth of Latinos within Christian higher education (CHE)? Alice Obenchain, William Johnson and Paul Dion propose that CHE institutions have a clan culture which prohibits others from entering the inner circles.[80] Another perspective is that there exist institutional practices that reflect continuing structural inequities, bias, racism, and the lack of commitment to diversity, equity, and inclusion.[81] Williams argues, "the conservative right tries to use the courts and legislative measures to thwart diversity efforts, [but] we need to redouble our commitment to increasing the enrollment and retention of ethnic and racial minorities in colleges, and to increasing the representation of both minorities and women in the science, technology,

77. Longman, Diversity Matters, 29.
78. Quoted in Longman, Diversity Matters, 33.
79. Núñez et al, Hispanic-Serving Institutions, 89.
80. Obenchain et al, "Institutional Types."
81. Smith, Diversity's Promise, 156.

engineering, and math fields (STEM), as well as in professional fields like law, medicine, and business."[82]

There is much work to be done within the field of diversity in Christian higher education, especially within executive leadership roles that seem to overlook Latinas even though there is a "greying" of current leaders, such as vice presidents and presidents.[83] Moffit states: "one glaring gap included the fact that there is virtually no research literature available that specifically addresses issues of racism and the impact they have on administrators of color who work at religiously-affiliated higher education institutions." Additionally, "very limited research has been conducted on the issues, challenges, and barriers of administrators of color who work at religiously-affiliated higher education institutions."[84] Although research is nonexistent for Latinx leaders in CHE, there exists a growing body of literature from public institutional research.[85]

Several dissertations have been published in the last ten years that address Latinx executive leadership in higher education. Leonard Savala asked four questions about Latinx experiences in predominately white institutions (PWIs) in his dissertation that produced five themes for consideration. The questions were:

1. How do Hispanic/Latino executives in higher education describe their leadership experiences at PWIs?

2. Why are so few Hispanic/Latinos leading within PWIs?

3. In what ways does ethnicity impact the decisions made at their institutions?

4. What strategies are beneficial to institutions looking to recruit and retain Hispanics/Latinos executives within PWIs?[86]

The five themes that emerged in Savala's research were: (1) the impact of ethnicity on decision-making, (2) inadequate educational pipeline, (3) lack of Latino leaders, (4) importance of mentoring, and (5) diversity and building an inclusive university.

According to Savala, there are other factors that have hindered the growth of Latinx leaders in higher education, including: (1) political connections and involvement, (2) affirmative action within a prospective

---

82. Williams, Strategic Diversity Leadership, 4.

83. Henck, "Walking the Tightrope."

84. Moffit, "A Narrative Study," 115–116.

85. Rodríguez et al,"Latino Educational Leadership," 136.

86. Savala, "The Experiences of Latino/a Executives," 129.

institution, (3) the context of the institution in which it finds itself, and (4) pressures from the Latinx community.[87] One of the major findings in this study was the importance of institutions creating pipelines for Latinx growth in leadership opportunities. Some important determinates that will help aspiring Latinx leaders to attain executive roles are seeking mentors, gaining a good grasp of their context, developing cross-cultural literacy, staying optimistic, and joining professional organizations.[88]

The lack of Latinx leadership presence seems to be a mystery for some, while others believe that the factors are clear. According to Gómez de Torres, the California Community College Chancellors office conducted a study in 2011 that revealed statewide "ethnicity headcount distribution by employee category of educational administration . . . 15.89% (316) Hispanics out of 1,989 education administrators."[89] Latinx presence seems to be more significant in community colleges nationwide (especially in California) than in four-year and graduate institutions.

Executive Latinx and other leaders of color equally face resistance and must overcome hurdles in higher education. Most Latinx leaders speak about facing racism, sexism, and opposition as they try to serve their institutions and grow through the ranks.[90] What has helped many Latinos in their leadership and tenure has been their relationship with their communities, *familias y culturas,* identity and spiritual capital.[91] Gloria Lopez identified another alarming issue that Latinx leaders need to overcome when being considered for leadership positions in higher education: "Latino candidates faced the conundrum of being expected to have the highest of qualifications and professional experiences while those qualities were simultaneously a disadvantage to Latinos as hiring decisions were made."[92] In other words, Latinx leaders have to wrestle with the notion of not being good enough when qualified, or even being considered over-qualified.

87. Savala, "The Experiences of Latino/a Executives, 142–144.

88. Savala, "The Experiences of Latina/o Executives," 147–148.

89. Gómez de Torres, "Latina Leaders in Higher Education," 20.

90. Lopez, "Pa'Lante! Toward the Presidency," 2021.

91. Lopez, "Pa'Lante! Toward the Presidency," 229–230.

92. Lopez, "Pa'Lante! Toward the Presidency," 26. A more robust explanation of this conundrum is presented later in the book.

LEADERSHIP, THEOLOGY AND MISSIOLOGY
IN A MULTICULTURAL SOCIETY

Latinx leaders in Christian higher education (CHE) come from various theological traditions. This section provides an introduction to the reader who may not be familiar with such traditions in order to make sense of the stories of Latinx leaders included later in the book. Juan Martínez declares, "not only have we had different social, cultural, and historical experiences, we also have had varied religious experiences."[93]

The church is in desperate need of intercultural leaders who are adaptable enough to serve a changing context.[94] The need is similar for leaders in CHE.[95] "Leadership is not about an individual or even a small group having great ideas and pulling a church into their vision. Leadership is about shaping an environment in which the people of God participate in the action-reflection cycle as they gain new capacities to discern what God is doing among and around them."[96] In the coming years, leaders simply must be contextual and have the capacity to serve fluently in diverse environments.

According to the U.S. Census (2015), there are more than 55 million Latinos in the U.S. Latinos are the largest minoritized group in the U.S., "but Latinos are also a reflection of the complex history of the United States in relationship to the Americas."[97] In other words, Latinos are the "Harvest of Empire."[98] Although Latinos have great numbers in the U.S., they still struggle economically, socially, and politically. Consequently, there is much work to be done for Latinx to flourish in this environment.

Many Latinx tasted the fierce Christianity of the U.S. via its profound abuses towards the Americas, stripping Latinos of their resources, family values, and livelihood. Contrary to contemporary political beliefs, the border crossed Mexico. De La Torre explains:

> Americans benefited from the nineteenth-century jingoist religious ideology of Manifest Destiny, which justified Anglo territorial expansion in North America. The massive land acquisitions from northern Mexico were based on a theology that

---

93. Juan Martínez, Walk with the People, 33.
94. Roxburgh and Romanuk, The Missional Leader, 105–106.
95. Poe, Christianity in the Academy, 73–74.
96. Branson and Martínez, Churches, Cultures, and Leadership, 57.
97. Martínez, Los Protestantes, 2.
98. Martínez, Los Protestantes, 2.

conceived the dominant Euroamerican culture as chosen by God
who destined Euroamericans to acquire the entire continent.[99]

These historic incidents seem to be yet unredeemed. And yet, this horri-
fying history has not necessarily barricaded Latinos from leadership and
ministry in the U.S. "Most Latino churches are multicultural: they have
people from many national, racial, and cultural backgrounds; though all are
identified as Latino."[100] Latinos have since ministered primarily from the
margins, at the grassroots level, serving the least of these. Although the first
Latino *evangélico* church was planted in New Mexico during the 1850's[101]
and Latino churches have continued to grow, "there is not one Latino com
munity, culturally speaking, nor only one Latino experience that defines all
U.S. Latinas."[102] In other words, Latinas bring a wealth of diverse experiences to their leadership and theology.

Many Latinx grow up in bicultural homes, multicultural contexts,
and speak several languages, creating an ideal environment for developing
cultural intelligence. Cultural intelligence can be defined as "the ability to
engage in a set of behaviors that uses skills (that is, language or interpersonal skills) and qualities (e.g., tolerance for ambiguity, flexibility) that are
tuned appropriately to the culture-based values and attitudes of the people
with whom one interacts."[103] The multicultural experience is a foundational
strength of Latinx leaders to the extent that it is their experience. An analysis of the narratives in the interviews shared later in this book demonstrates
not only the presence of the factors contributing to cultural intelligence, but
also the validity of the assumption that these Latinx leaders embodied the
responsiveness and agility necessary to create safe spaces for the increasingly diverse student bodies in their schools.

A primary justification for Latinx leadership in CHE is the reality
that Latinx leaders understand the diverse cultures and identities of their
students. Martínez states that Latino identity is polycentric and fluid. He
describes seven diverse identities Latinos may relate to within their own
culture and in correlation with the majority culture in the U.S.:

1. Nuclear Latino—are immersed within their own Latino culture and
   have limited contact or influence from the majority culture.

99. De La Torre, The Politics of Jesús, 38–39.

100. Martínez, Los Protestantes,129.

101. Martínez, Los Protestantes, 69.

102. Martínez, Los Protestantes, 67.

103. Peterson, Cultural Intelligence, 89.

2. Bicultural Latino—live in-between Latino and majority culture at all times.

3. Marginal Latino—identify with their culture from time to time, but are mostly influenced by the majority culture.

4. Fleeing Latino—do not want anything to do with their Latinism and are confident that incorporating into the Anglo culture is the best thing for them.

5. Returning Latino—discover their Latino culture and try to reinforce it.

6. Assimilated Latino—know mildly their Latino culture through history but are most comfortable in the majority culture.

7. Another culture Latino—usually marry into another marginalized culture (like African American) and assimilate into this newer culture.[104]

These Latinx represent the diversity that is within the Latinx community. According to Martínez, there are some Latinx that would be inclined to assimilate to the Eurocentric way of doing things, versus others that would resist it or be willing to work interculturally or multiculturally.

According to Bordas, "Multicultural leadership is an inclusive approach and philosophy that incorporates the influences, practices, and values of diverse cultures in a respectful and productive manner. Multicultural leadership resonates with many cultures and encourages diverse people to actively engage, contribute, and tap their potential."[105] In sum, as we will demonstrate later in this book, multicultural leadership and ministry are an intrinsic element in the experience of the Latinx leaders since these leaders represent "a blend of races and cultures from various regions of Latin America, but they are also natives of this country."[106]

According to Jorge Lara-Braud, U.S. Latinx spirituality is "the response of life and the sacred."[107] Latinas come from representations of Spain, Puerto Rico, Mexico, the Caribbean, and Latin America. More than thirty-five centuries ago, civilizations from Indian roots have been the birth of this unique blend of people from "Indian mothers" to their "European fathers."[108] U.S. Latinas bear all the glory of their ancestors, and many integrate the added component of being a U.S. citizen.

104. Martínez, Walk with the People, 20–22.
105. Bordas, Salsa, Soul, and Spirit, 8.
106. Ramírez-Johnson and Hernández, Avance, 9.
107. Lara-Braud, "Hispanic-American Spirituality," 89–90.
108. Lara-Braud, "Hispanic-American Spirituality, 90.

U.S. Latinas see the United States as "a land for refuge," but for some it is a land of persecution.[109] For example, "when U.S. Hispanics (Puerto Rican-Americans in particular) visit families in Puerto Rico, many are told that they are not real *Puertorriquenos* (Puerto Ricans), while back home many are told to go back to the Island from which they came."[110] The younger generation seems to be fighting back for their Latino-American rights. This may be the reason why Latinx have adopted the attitude of César Chavez in proclaiming "*si se puede*" (yes we can!).

Since Latinas hold multiple religious affiliations, and may identify as Catholic, Protestant, nondenominational or interdenominational (or of no faith), theological reflection may be a hybrid of all views.[111] Lara-Braud writes that this makes "U.S. Hispanics aliens in the promised-land."[112] No one is exempt from the lenses with which they do their theology.[113] This seems to get more complicated when the added denominational, cultural, historical, and societal measures are in place. U.S. Latina theology faces the same complexities. To add to the mixture of Latinx circles, some Latinx are bilingual, while some only speak English or Spanish (or even Spanglish).[114] Most Latinx in the U.S. live in urban centers, have predominately low incomes, and are striving to survive; this may give them a unique theological reason to sympathize with the poor and the marginalized.[115]

Many Latinas have come to the U.S. to live in what they believe is the "promised land," while others have come with the mindset that it is the land of the free, and the land of opportunity. Numerous Latinx have had culture shock, trauma, and other problems when faced with the realities this country has provided.[116] For several U.S. Latinas, the hope was to come to the U.S. for political freedom, better work, and a promising future. Many realized that the "promised land" was a promise for some, but for many it was a daunting nightmare.[117]

The fainting reality was, and at times still is, that Latinx are seen as "aliens" in the United States. As Juan F. Martínez declares, "Latinos are also

---

109. Lara-Braud, "Hispanic-American Spirituality," 98–99.

110. Isasi-Diaz and Segovia, Hispanic Latino Theology, 137.

111. Lara-Braud, "Hispanic-American Spirituality," 98–99.

112. Lara-Braud, "Hispanic-American Spirituality," 99.

113. Isasi-Diaz and Segovia, Hispanic Latino Theology, 134.

114. Spanglish is a term commonly used in the Latinx community to describe speaking Spanish and English simultaneously as one unified language.

115. Isasi-Diaz and Segovia, Hispanic Latino Theology, 135.

116. Isasi-Diaz and Segovia, Hispanic Latino Theology, 24.

117. Isasi-Diaz and Segovia, Hispanic Latino Theology, 24.

a reflection of the complex history of the United States in relationship to the Americas . . . the United States has also intervened [negatively] politically, economically, and militarily in various parts of the Americas throughout its history. Latin America is perceived as the United States' backyard."[118] Countless Latinx immigrants were faced with the harsh reality that the U.S. was in part responsible for the political nightmare back home. Father Romero of El Salvador asked the U.S. to stop selling and sending weapons to his country, which eventually got him murdered while conducting mass. Ruth A. Tucker describes how Orlando Costas expressed his experience in the U.S.: "I came face to face with Anglo-Saxon culture in its worst form . . . the puritanical value system . . . the shameless defense and justification of racism . . . and the triumphalist belief in the divine (manifest) destiny of the United States."[119]

The alienation observed by Martínez underlies a trend toward liberationist perspectives of theology among Latinx in the U.S. Gilbert R. Cadena writes that "U.S. Hispanics do liberation theology through their experiences confronting patriarchy and sexism, as well as racism and classism."[120] According to Cadena, "U.S. Hispanics have left Catholicism to Protestantism at the rate of about sixty thousand annually, since the 1980s."[121] Cadena proclaims that Latinx have received the poorest education; lowest-paying jobs, and live in the poorest areas of their cities. In education, Latinas in the U.S. fall lower in "attainment, more than Euro-Americans, African-Americans, and Asian-Americans."[122] These characteristics of U.S. Latinos have a significant impact on Latinx communities, as they play out in theological reflection and sociocultural activities, particularly in higher education.[123]

Robert Chao Romero describes the Latinx diverse community of faith as the Brown Church:

> a prophetic ecclesial community of [Latinx] that has contested racial and social injustice in Latin America and the United States for the past five hundred years. As such, Brown Church is a multivalent category, encompassing ethnic, historical, theological, spiritual, and sociopolitical dimensions.[124]

118. Martínez, Los Protestantes, 2.
119. Tucker, From Jerusalem to Irian Jaya, 447.
120. Quoted in Isasi-Diaz and Segovia, Hispanic Latino Theology, 174.
121. Isasi-Diaz and Segovia, Hispanic Latino Theology, 175.
122. Isasi-Diaz and Segovia, Hispanic Latino Theology, 174.
123. Isasi-Diaz and Segovia, Hispanic Latino Theology, 174.
124. Romero, Brown Church, 11.

Romero further explains that the Brown Church has developed what is known as "Brown Theology." Brown Theology, while not ignoring the imperative tenets of salvation and heaven, does not leave out the biblical values of justice and the social dimensions of Jesus' redemption.[125] In other words, Latinx theology is holistic, encompassing both the personal and public lives of the faithful. These theological constructs will be explored further.

CONCLUSION

We have so far presented a broad view of literature pertaining to Latinx in general, and Latinx in higher education in particular. Identifying, as we have, some crucial differences in leadership and specifically Christian leadership literature, we then examined Latinx students in higher education, executive leaders in higher education, and provided an introduction to Latinx theology. Our examination of these Latinx particularities is foundational to understanding the experiences of Latinx leaders in CHE, because of the vast experiences and traditions that the Latinx community epitomizes.

It has been said that Latinas must work twice as hard to be considered half as good.[126] I examined this assertion by investigating and interviewing five executive Latinx leaders in the CCCU, since present Latinx leadership research in the CCCU is nonexistent. The interviews conducted for this book will shed some light and provide a platform for future research on diversity issues pertaining to the experiences of executive Latinx leaders in CHE. To understand the context, I next move to present the current landscape of CHE and how it impacts Latinx leaders and people of color more broadly.

---

125. Romero, Brown Church, 12.

126. This is a commonly known saying within the Latinx community in CHE.

3

The Current Landscape of Christian Higher Education

In 1954 an event occurred that would profoundly affect evangelicals' views on race: the Supreme Court's decision in Brown v. Board of Education. This landmark decision mandating school desegregation launched one of the defining civil rights battles of the era. In response, many evangelicals took their children out of public school rather than have them attend with African Americans. Churches and other evangelical organizations founded "segregation academies," private religious schools that were tax-exempt.[1]

In this next chapter, I invite you to chart with me the current landscape of Christian higher education (CHE) as it relates to diversity (or the lack thereof) with a specific focus on the Council of Christian Colleges and Universities (CCCU). We will begin by presenting concepts of race as a foundation from which to understand diversity, equity, and inclusion (DEI) efforts of CHE. Furthermore, I try to organize my thoughts around the realities of colonialism and the ramifications of its economic engine. In other words, from the global colonial enterprise we inherited the social and theological construct of race, which works at the intersections of economics, politics, and the Christian faith. This is an essential step in laying a foundation from

---

1. Butler, White Evangelical Racism, 44–45.

which to understand how theology and missiology are observed in practice in conservative schools, represented by the leaders' narratives in this book.

I then move to introduce relevant historical factors in the history of CHE and the birth of the CCCU. Due to social changes in the U.S. and evolving perceptions of Christianity, colleges and universities began to move away from religious ideologies and move towards nonsectarian perspectives. However, it is evident by the stories shared later in this book that these colleges and universities still struggle with the dominance of White privilege. The theology and idea of White Jesus as portrayed in the work of Alexander Jun, Tabatha Jolivet, Allison Ash, and Christopher Collins[2] is a widespread reality in the campus climate in CCCU schools as observed by the leaders in this study. My concluding thoughts touch on the importance of the connection between the church and the CCCU, and its contributions to developing leaders for society.

RACE: POLITICS, ECONOMICS, AND THE CHRISTIAN RELIGION

In the following section I use the method of critical discourse analysis to showcase the connections of diverse scholars in a transdisciplinary dialogue synthesizing concerns common to the narratives and interviews of Latinx leaders in the research. More specifically, I research and present issues at the intersection of politics, economics, and the Christian faith as these issues pertain to Christian higher education (CHE) and the experiences of people of color within this context. This interdisciplinary section is important due to the inseparable nature of the equity and inclusion concerns the interviewees shared and the connection of these concerns to the CHE enterprise.

In United States politics there are two major or primary parties—the Democratic and Republican parties. The general American public today would identify conservative notions as largely aligned with the Republicans and liberalism with the Democrats. However, both parties have changed their ideologies, positions, and systems over time.[3] Research reveals that the Republican party initiated its contemporary conservative agenda around 1979—1980 surrounding the election of Ronald Reagan.[4] According to Jun et al, "racial separatism was at the inception of the Religious right movement, but it was masked by the moral issue of abortion." Jun et al further

2. Jun et al, White Jesus.

3. Lewis, Ideas of Power, 2.

4. Brooks et al, Understanding American Politics, 85; Kruse, One Nation Under God, 281; Jun et al, White Jesus, 48; Djupe and Claassen, The Evangelical Crackup?, 49.

state: "the hypocrisy of the Religious Right's support of Reagan centered around a misalignment with two key areas that were of interest among White evangelicals during the 1980 election: profamily and pro-life."[5] In other words, evangelicals began to stack their vote and influence solely on a scripted perception of these two moral issues.

Another perspective is that the White evangelical voter is not necessarily concerned about moral or value issues after all, evidenced by "the poor fit between Trump's biography and the assumption that morality politics drive evangelical political behavior,"[6] although many have compared Trump to King Cyrus of the Old Testament.[7] On the contrary, Trump's election revealed a group of voters that will combat any federal effort to tackle persistent problems of racial inequity."[8] This is also apparent since 81 percent of "Trumpvangelicals" voted for Donald Trump in the 2016 election and 75 percent voted for him in 2020.[9] The main point here is that the Republican party is more inclined to swing towards a bloc of issues that rely on systemic racism, rather than voting according to the values agenda that is so popular among its public. Concerning White evangelicals and their politics, Anthea Butler contends:

> Evangelicalism is not a simply religious group at all. Rather, it is a nationalistic political movement whose purpose is to support the hegemony of white Christian men over and against the flourishing of others. To put it more baldly, evangelicalism is an Americanized Christianity born in the context of white Christian slaveholders. It sanctified and justified segregation, violence, and racial proscription. Slavery and racism permeate evangelicalism, and as much as evangelicals like to protest that they are color-blind, their theologies, cultures, and beliefs are anything but.[10]

Systemic racism did not start with Donald Trump in 2016, although it may have been emboldened through his unabashed xenophobic comments towards minoritized communities. Despite this, "race has been at the heart of political controversy over equality in America since before the Revolutionary War."[11] As an example, the historical Voting Rights Act was limited

5. Jun et al, White Jesus, 48.

6. Djupe and Claassen, The Evangelical Crackup?, 50.

7. Butler, White Evangelical Racism, 2.

8. Djupe and Claassen, The Evangelical Crackup?, 50.

9. Sherwood, "White Evangelical Christians."

10. Butler, White Evangelical Racism, 138.

11. Brooks et al, Understanding American Politics, 231.

to English language-only voting materials, effectively restricting the Latinx vote, and yet still today similar strategies are used to block the majority-minority from their right to vote.[12] The loss of Donald Trump's presidential bid in 2020 has provoked fourteen states to enact twenty-two new laws making it difficult to vote by mail or absentee ballot.[13] Many believe this is a conservative strategy to restrict the vote of people of color and other minoritized groups in America.[14]

Other political tactics have been employed by the majority culture to suppress the advancement of a dignified life for people of color. Some people of color have been submitted to long working hours with very little pay through "dual wage systems,"[15] substandard working conditions, inhumane living areas, slavery in many forms, and the oppression and exploitation of women, and other minoritized groups. The criminal justice system has worked against people of color to the extent that the majority incarcerated today are black and brown bodies.[16] "In 1972, America's correctional facilities held some 333,000 prisoners. By 2000, the inmate population had soared to 1,890,000."[17] According to the National Association for the Advancement of Colored People (NAACP):

- There are 3 million people in jail and prison today, far outpacing population growth and crime. Between 1980 and 2015, the number of people incarcerated increased from roughly 500,000 to 2.2. million.

- Despite making up close to 5 percent of the global population, the U.S. has nearly 25 percent of the world's prison population.

- 32 percent of the US population is represented by African Americans and Hispanics, compared to 56 percent of the US incarcerated population being represented by African Americans and Hispanics.

- If African Americans and Hispanics were incarcerated at the same rates as whites, prison and jail populations would decline by almost 40 percent.[18]

There is a major issue with our criminal justice system in the U.S.

12. Malavé and Giordani, Latino Stats, 25.
13. Boschma, "Fourteen States."
14. Boschma, "Fourteen States."
15. Ortiz, An African American and Latinx History, 125.
16. Ortiz, An African American and Latinx History, 167.
17. Ortiz, An African American and Latinx History, 167.
18. NAACP, "Criminal Justice Factsheet."

The presidential election of 2016 demonstrated where the United States was situated concerning intercultural relations. Donald Trump won the election by proclaiming that he would "make America great again" (MAGA). While MAGA excited parts of the majority culture of the U.S., it was appalling for the majority-minority. As De La Torre explains: "the call to 'make America great again' is a demand to return to an era where my brown skin would have relegated me to mopping the floors at my graduate school rather than teaching in its classrooms."[19] Trump's election to the presidency partly on the basis of his promising to build a wall seems to indicate that the U.S. is not yet a "post-racial" society.[20]

Paul Ortiz argues that the notion of MAGA is intentionally oblivious to the history of the imperialism and emancipatory internationalism of the U.S.[21] Ortiz reasons that one would have to ignore slavery, military dominance across seas, and other capitalistic ventures that allowed the U.S. to gain the land that it claimed as manifest destiny,[22] while additionally ignoring the disastrous effects of bullying throughout the global south. While much of the majority culture may have amnesia to the historical atrocities that still occur, people of color, the marginalized, and other vulnerable populations are reminded everyday of their second-class citizenship in the "land of the free."

Nonetheless, as previously stated, this did not start with Trump's presidency; systemic racism and inequity have always pervaded U.S. politics, economics, and religion. Robert P. Jones contends that this has always been the face of White Christian America (WCA).[23] WCA is related to the late term White Anglo Saxon Protestant (WASP), which according to Jones, is used to portray the U.S. cultural and religious "center." The term WCA, like WASP, has its roots in northern Europe and its religiosity situates itself within Protestantism; however, Jones believes that WCA has broader applicability than WASP for these two reasons: (1) it includes mainline Christians and evangelicals alike, and (2) it is a more inclusive and neutral term. In other words, WCA's main project remains to keep all things "White." Although mainliners would be more inclusive and liberal in certain theological circles than evangelicals, White Christian Americans of all affiliations still struggle with racial bigotry and intercultural equity.

---

19. De La Torre, Burying White Privilege, 13.

20. The Trump support from Latinx is addressed later through testimonios of the Latinx interviewed for this book.

21. Ortiz, An African American and Latinx History, 1.

22. Ortiz, An African American and Latinx History, 105.

23. Jones, The End of White Christian America, 30–38.

This was showcased when Barack Obama was elected as the President of the United States. His main critics argued through frames of both race and religion about his citizenship, mainly focusing on the idea that he was neither White nor Christian.[24] Furthermore, Obama definitely did not qualify as either WASP or WCA. These critics, these "agents of intolerance" as Jones calls them, were indignant about the many challenges WCA was encountering. Jones explains:

> The Obama presidency provided a unique focal point for many white Christian voters, who already felt as if familiar cultural touchstones were disappearing at every turn. Shifting social norms, declining religious affiliation, changing demographics, and a struggling economy—all were embodied in one powerful symbol: a black man in the White House.[25]

Obama's presidency helped the U.S. in terms of cultural responsiveness, but there continues to be segregation and division, to say the least. According to Jones, there persist three realities that segregate U.S. citizens: (1) geographic segregation, (2) the majority of white people do not have intimate relationships with people of color, and (3) no U.S. institution exists that is strategically situated to deal with issues of systemic and social segregation.[26] The church is still one of the least well-positioned to assist in intercultural matters, reflecting that Sunday is still the most segregated day of the week.[27]

WCA has been the main leader in U.S. oppressive history. Within this historical account, the Southern Baptists (SBC) have been most responsible for racist conflicts through religious nuances.[28] The SBC was created before the Civil War via its commitment to continuing slavery. In 1845, the American Baptist Foreign Mission Society declared that any slave owner would be disqualified from missionary service. Therefore, the SBC was created for southern Baptist church leaders to continue their capitalism and missionary calling simultaneously.[29] However, denominational splits over slavery were not unique to Baptists, since most White mainline denominations including Northern Methodists and Southern Methodists also separated in 1845.[30]

This type of hypocrisy from large parts of the church led theologians and missiologists like James H. Cone and Orlando Costas to write against

24. Jones, The End of White Christian America, 80–81.
25. Jones, The End of White Christian America, 97.
26. Jones, The End of White Christian America, 155–156.
27. Brooks et al, Understanding American Politics, 242.
28. Jones, The End of White Christian America, 167–168.
29. Jones, The End of White Christian America, 168.
30. Jones, White Too Long, 6.

the 'white' Jesus and show a more holistic gospel that could liberate and not continue oppressing the marginalized. Cone specified, "unfortunately, white theologians, then and since, have typically ignored the problem of race, or written and spoken about it without urgency, not regarding it as critical for theology and ethics."[31] One reason for this absence of empathy from the White church and its theologians concerning issues of race can be attributed to the notion that it is not necessary. Intercultural dynamics and racial issues have been ignored by WCA leadership primarily because it is not a prominent issue for them. As the old proverb goes, "it's hard to put yourself in someone else's shoes when yours fit just fine." As Cone declared, "in the lynching era, between 1880 to 1940, white Christians lynched nearly five thousand black men and women in a manner with obvious echoes of the Roman crucifixion of Jesus. Yet these 'Christians' did not see the irony or contradiction in their actions."[32]

Even today, WCA does not see the irony of their actions towards people of color. Since 2016, a wall has begun to be built to keep Mexican "criminals" out of a land that previously belonged to them, immigrant children have been wrenched away from their parents, people of color continue to be murdered on the streets by the police and incarcerated at a higher level than those from the majority culture, and government funding gets disbursed inequitably. When Hurricane Maria devastated the island of Puerto Rico, Trump was seen tossing paper towels to desperate islanders as if he were shooting basketball hoops. This type of behavior has led many people of color to doubt the Christian faith that the majority culture broadcasts.[33] De La Torre emphasizes:

> Our quest is for a Jesus not captured by the dominant Eurocentric culture. The White Jesus is damning to the disenfranchised. The world's disposed search for a Jesus who resonates specifically with those excluded by the hegemonic Eurocentric Christianity. The Jesus of the United States of America to whom Donald Trump and his apologists bend their knees can never save the disenfranchised who are consigned to the underside of Whiteness. The crucial first step toward saying yes to God, yes to salvation, yes to liberation, and yes to our communities is to say no to oppression masked by nationalist Christianity draped in the Stars and Stripes.[34]

31. Cone, Cross and Lynching Tree, 52.
32. Cone, Cross and Lynching Tree, 31.
33. De La Torre, Burying White Privilege, 13.
34. De La Torre, Burying White Privilege, 13.

In essence, what De La Torre is saying is that there must be a reckoning of how politics has in some ways hijacked faith in the U.S. and has sidelined the "least of these." Jesus came to set the captives free, yet the majority culture of the U.S. continues to oppress Latinx and other people of color through their political bias. I find it hard to side with a group of people who claim to be "pro-life," yet have no issues separating thousands of brown children (in 2019 the count was around 69,550) from their families in the present Southern border crisis.[35]

ECONOMICS AND RELIGION

The U.S. has always attempted to make a profit at the expense of human rights and dignity.[36] One of the main revenue generators of the country in the eighteenth and nineteenth century was the Atlantic slave trade.[37] While the majority culture plays innocent regarding its exceptionalism, history tells a different story. As Ortiz declares, "the slave plantation was the engine of early economic growth in the Americas, the force behind the rise of global markets in tobacco, sugar, molasses, dyestuffs, cotton, and other commodities."[38] The American Revolution was itself a conflict fed by efforts to retain slavery in the U.S,[39] and the Civil War occurred because "the society valued profits over Black humanity."[40]

The slave trade was blessed by popes and slave ships were often accompanied by Protestant and Catholic clergy.[41] The increase of a nation's "bottom line" allowed leaders to ignore the immense human disgrace of slavery, and once again profit was the god of the nation.[42] Voyages to the New World and so-called new discoveries were done in the name of the Lord, but really in the name of the god—mammon. Portugal, France, England, Holland, and Spain were some of the first countries to gravitate to this global capitalistic system of dehumanizing black and brown bodies.[43]

Jesus once declared, "No one can serve two masters. Either you will hate the one and love the other, or you will be devoted to the one and

---

35. Sherman et al, "U.S. Held Record Number of Migrant Children."
36. Ortiz, An African American and Latinx History, 3.
37. Sechrest et al, Can "White" People Be Saved?, 27.
38. Ortiz, An African American and Latinx History, 12.
39. Ortiz, An African American and Latinx History, 14.
40. Ortiz, An African American and Latinx History, 62–63.
41. Hopkins, Being Human, 135.
42. Hopkins, Being Human, 135.
43. Hopkins, Being Human, 136.

despise the other. You cannot serve both God and money" (Matt 6:24, NIV). Yet, this is what seemed to drive the colonial enterprise—greed. Dwight N. Hopkins asserts:

> Race in missiological endeavors consisted of the crown (colonial government), the cannon (the military), commerce (the growth of capitalism in Europe and North America), civilization (the supremacy of white culture), and the cross (the imposition of the noninclusive Jesus truth of Jesus Christ). As it tore down barriers and seduced its victims, the power of colonial Jesus violently attacked the religious identities and cultural aesthetics and ancient powers of indigenous peoples throughout the globe.[44]

Clergy were often on payroll in West Africa for this global capitalistic enterprise. Alongside these ministers worked many businesspeople, military personnel directing installations for trade, and other figures of authority and power. These worked in concert to establish mission stations as outposts of Westernization, converts into officers of Europeanization, and evangelization as acculturation.[45] In other words, many people worked with clergy to westernize Africans.

In speaking of the Christian faith, it is difficult to obviate its ties to slavery and its dependency on this economic apparatus. The dark history of the church serving as the pimp for black and brown bodies across the ocean for a profit seems to be a hard truth for Christians to acknowledge. Distortions in theological views, like the Hamitic curse, made it possible for Europeans to believe that dark people were serving their due portion from God,[46] and that the exploitation of such people as the will of Jesus for them. Hopkins further states:

> Christianization, civilization, and commercialization forged a distinct worldview and purpose: to force black folks to wear European clothing and adopt white culture (hence, the aesthetic accent), to educate Aboriginals into speaking English and adopt "Christian" names (hence, the identity move), and to imbue them with a Protestant (capitalist) work ethic to remake them into laborers on their stolen lands (hence, removing their power by revoking their land-ownership and mandating a Christian necessity to surrender their labor power for the priest, the property owner, and the politician).[47]

44. Hopkins, Being Human, 148.
45. Jesse Mugambi in Hopkins, Being Human, 149.
46. Hopkins, Being Human, 155.
47. Hopkins, Being Human, 156.

Theological institutions have been employing a Christian imagination for some time now. According to Willie Jennings,

> The Christian theological imagination was woven into processes of colonial dominance. Other peoples and their ways of life had to adapt, become fluid, even morph into the colonial order of things, and such a situation drew Christianity and its theologians inside habits of mind and life that internalized and normalized that order of things.[48]

The old world entered (in colonial fashion) the new worlds of Asia, Africa, and the Americas and assumed authority over natives, stripping them of their identity, culture, and traditions. The colonialist claimed land and people, all in the name of God.

Modern Christianity suffers from a diseased social imagination.[49] This altered social imagination desires to be colorblind and to forget or outright ignore the historical ramifications produced by colonialization throughout the world. Capitalism became a racist system that used politics, the Christian faith, whiteness, and power to make differentiations among people. As missionaries moved into the new worlds and established the crown and cross, the story was that they were anchoring the faith by saving the heathens who needed to be rescued from their ignorance; a Christian story that has been recycled throughout the ages.[50]

The European expansion from Portugal and Spain provoked a daunting disruption with "space and bodies, land and identity," which gave formation to identity in modernity.[51] According to Jennings, "the ordering of existence from white to black signifies much more than the beginnings of racial formation on a global scale: it is an architecture that signals displacement. Herein lies the deepest theological problem."[52] People have been ordered by color and economic standing ever since. Whiteness emerges as superior to all and the whiter a person's complexion, the better off they would be in the pecking order of humanity. This pervasive Christian imagination has distorted society's view of people who have been created in God's image and likeness. As Jennings declares, "This effect begins with positioning Christian identity fully within European (white) identity."[53]

---

48. Jennings, The Christian Imagination, 8.
49. Jennings, The Christian Imagination, 9.
50. Jennings, The Christian Imagination, 20.
51. Jennings, The Christian Imagination, 24.
52. Jennings, The Christian Imagination, 25.
53. Jennings, The Christian Imagination, 33.

The after-marks of such Whiteness have normed White theology.[54] J. Kameron Carter argues that theology is not necessarily the problem of the day, but that the issue is Whiteness in particular.[55] This Whiteness of the West also separated Christianity from its Jewish roots,[56] reducing it to a "conquest faith" of the majority culture of the U.S. Carter prophetically offers a new way forward, set apart from the privilege of the elite and the White scholastic norm:

> [I call] for a new habitus, a new Christian theological-intellectual practice, one that arises from the everyday practices of the very people the forgetting of whom is the condition of the scholastic universes of "homo academics." Their lives and the practices through which they negotiate their real worlds of pain and suffering and life and death must become the locus or the disposition out of which theology does its work. . .In connection with the poor one, at the various sites of the underside of modernity, and, in short, from the places of suffering—this is the locus from which theology must be renewed.[57]

Christianity has a legacy that is too often ignored. As previously detailed, in speaking of the Christian faith, it is difficult to overlook its ties to slavery and its dependency on this economic system. It is also worth mentioning again that the church of Jesus Christ in the U.S. cannot continue to ignore its responsibility in the creation of race as a social construct and class system in American society. It is time for White Christians in the U.S. "to reckon with the racism of [their] past and the willful amnesia of [their] present."[58] Ignoring injustices or trying to sweep these issues under the rug will not solve our present problems. Presently, in 2021, there is a push in states like Florida and Arkansas to make teaching Critical Race Theory (CRT) illegal, along with the historical facts surrounding issues of slavery and racism in America.[59] The argument for these new laws is that CRT teaches children to hate America, that the U.S. is fundamentally racist, and its laws uphold White supremacy, and that all White people are racist. I believe that the real issue is that White supremacy and unearned White Christian privilege, power, and profit are being challenged and called to account.[60] White nor-

54. Carter, Race, 157.
55. Carter, Race, 372.
56. Carter, Race, 376.
57. Carter, Race, 374.
58. Jones, White Too Long, 6.
59. Dutton, Jack, "Critical Race Theory."
60. Butler, White Evangelical Racism, 145.

mativity is no longer accepted as the standard, and its dominance is being questioned through the lived experiences of others. White theology is going through a considerably overdue examination.

This theology of Whiteness that saturates the White evangelical church in the U.S. seems to have much influence, as will be evident in the CCCU schools in the narratives of this book. The rest of this chapter will deal with how this theology of Whiteness has played out in CHE and its efforts towards diversity, equity, and inclusion. But first, we will turn to examine Whiteness in CHE, since this is a prevailing issue that people of color navigate.

WHITE PRIVILEGE, WHITENESS, AND WHITE DOMINANCE

It would be very difficult to separate the systemic issues of race in the U.S. from the Christian faith and conquest, the politics of economics, and the notion of Whiteness that ties them all together. As De La Torre argues:

> Notwithstanding of how genuine and sympathetic white Christians may be, the way they have been taught to read the Bible advocates classism, racism. . .and misogyny, making them heirs to those who previously used Holy Writ to persecute disenfranchised racial and ethnic groups. Like their spiritual ancestors who perpetrated genocide to "save" heathens and fulfill their Manifest Destiny of occupying stolen land, white Christians continue to commit outrages today, in spite of the sincerity of their faith.[61]

Although the Naturalization Act of 1790 offered citizenship to free White people,[62] which made Whiteness a legal status in the U.S.,[63] the type of Whiteness to which I refer here started after the industrial revolution.[64] Immigrants discovered that upon entering the U.S, their economic and social status was elevated if they could somehow affiliate themselves with White people (or Whiteness). In other words, it was beneficial to move away from the notion of "foreigner, stranger or illegal" and "brown and black" and closer to a White nationalist ideology. As Christopher S. Collins and Alexander Jun declare, "Whiteness is a socially constructed status that is

61. De La Torre, Burying White Privilege, 42.

62. Ortiz, An African American and Latinx History, 20.

63. Joshi, White Christian Privilege, 110.

64. Nkomo, "Historical Originals of Ethnic (White) Privilege," 392; Rodríguez, Racism and God-Talk, 3.

often assumed to be biological as it relates to skin color. Race is undoubtedly a social construct, as various periods in history show that Whiteness was an achievable status. For example, consider the Italians and Irish as early immigrants to the US and their ability to achieve a generically White status."[65] The irony of this is that while some could assimilate into Whiteness, within the same country African Americans were considered 3/5 human beings in the very Constitution of the United States.[66]

This type of culture was led by the capitalist owner and distributed to the employment force. Not only were unfair work conditions given to people of color, but they also had to use different restrooms that were often less than ideal for human beings.[67] According to Stella Nkomo:

> Blacks were used as a counterpoint by the white working class to come to terms with their own acceptance of the regimented control they were subjected to under industrial capitalism. Whiteness was the means by which formerly indentured servants who had become lowly white workers in the factories and mills could assert their identity as truly "freemen" in juxtaposition to the enslaved black.[68]

White privilege gave certain individuals the opportunity to attain unearned profit, privilege, and power,[69] growth in leadership and influence, property ownership and better-paying jobs; while money has always been the central focal point in the religion of White supremacy.[70] This has created a huge economic divide within the social construction of a race. When speaking about economics and notions of race, Hopkins declares:

> An economic discourse in racial theory takes on the ties between monopolization of wealth and disproportionate possession of income on the part of white citizens. The concertation of great wealth belongs to a very small group of exclusive white families who influence, if not dominate, every major institution in America. Thus, the majority of white Americans lack control of wealth. However, even in matters of income, white citizens, in total, control income out of proportion to their abilities if they were not skewed, racialized economic playing field. In other

---

65. Collins and Jun, White Out, 2.

66. Collins and Jun, White Out, 2; Ragone, Everything American Government Book, 10.

67. Nkomo, "Historical Originals of Ethnic (White) Privilege," 392.

68. Nkomo, "Historical Originals of Ethnic (White) Privilege," 393.

69. De La Torre, Decolonizing Christianity, 87.

70. Robinson, Race and Theology, 93.

words, one of the unstated public criteria for access to wealth and income is being a white person.[71]

With the dawn of the industrial revolution came displacement for Native Americans, discrimination for the Latinx population as half-citizens, and dehumanization for African Americans and Asians. A categorization of people was developed, and White supremacy reigned in colonial fashion. It is important for Christians to recognize that this separation of people through skin color and economic status has contributed to painful divisions today in the U.S. church and Christian higher education (CHE). This history of categorization and division has created systemic racism and continues to be perpetuated by White evangelicals.[72] In other words, physical differences have historically been used to classify people through race, which has allowed for a view of inferiority applied to those who are not considered White, "revealing an irrational, even pathological commitment to the ideal of white superiority."[73]

People of color have historically had to work in substandard conditions. Besides working in these types of environments, being underpaid and given minimal opportunities to succeed has been the norm for the majority-minority culture in the U.S. In other words, the playing field has never been level for all. Many minoritized communities have had to work twice as hard to get less than their White colleagues, and women continue to get paid less than men in similar positions. Speaking about the complications of White privilege, and the "double work" people of color must do to be considered half as good, De La Torre articulates:

> To occupy a body of color within the United States is a continuous challenge. Not a day passes when I am not reminded. I'm an outsider and that the space I occupy was never intended for me. To occupy this space, I (and all people of color) am forced to be fluent in Eurocentric philosophy and theology. To reject the worldview of those who excluded the colonized, attempting to construct my theological view on my own cultural context, is to risk being dismissed as unscholarly or exotic. No institution of higher education within the United States would have granted me a PhD if I were not fluent in Hegel, Heidegger, or Habbermas. And yet my white colleagues are deemed rigorous scholars without ever having to read Sor Juana Inés de la Cruz, José Martí, or Miguel de Unamuno. I must be fluent in Eurocentric thought

71. Hopkins, Being Human, 121–122.
72. Robinson, Race and Theology, 86.
73. Rodríguez, Racism and God-Talk, 54.

and knowledgeable about the contributions made by scholars relegated to the underside of the academy. While this double-consciousness gives me a broader and more rigorous grasp of reality than my white colleagues have, still a large number of those colleagues insist that affirmative action was responsible for my professorship.[74]

De La Torre presents valid points about people of color in the U.S. having to develop a double and triple consciousness to be fluent in multiple worlds. White evangelicals have never had to do such a thing because of their positions of White privilege and power. Whiteness has permeated all systems of the world; from education to business and the corporate world, and specifically the church and CHE in the U.S. Eurocentric principles became the standard for all to learn and navigate. People from the margins understand that there are unwritten and unspoken rules to follow, and if you do not follow the rules, you may be passed by for another person who submits or conforms to White rules, including people of the same race or culture.

White privilege and dominance in the U.S. have developed into a social system that benefits the majority culture. It has been established as an architecture of the mind (and in religion and education), where minoritized communities have limited choices and are assigned to certain spaces. This racialized architecture identifies who is in or out of the main group, and is a good predictor of who will be successful.[75] Collins and Jun argue that the "White architecture of the mind is a term and an analogy to highlight that the mind is a result of a set of blueprints, constructions, walls, doors, windows, and pathways that influence and predispose individuals to react based on a systemic logic that was socially constructed."[76] In other words, White privilege provides access to members of the majority group to access upward mobility and strategic opportunities.

The authors argue that White privilege comes from the architecture of a White Jesus, which has been accepted as normative White theology stemming from colonialist origins. Alexander Jun et al. describe White Jesus as:

> a socially constructed apparatus—that operates stealthily as a veneer for patriarchal White supremist, capitalist, and imperialist sociopolitical, cultural, and economic agendas. White Jesus was constructed by combining empire, colorism, racism, education, and religion—and the byproduct is a distortion that reproduces violence in epistemic and physical ways. We distinguish

74. De La Torre, Burying White Privilege, 43–44.
75. Collins and Jun, White Out, 3.
76. Collins and Jun, White Out, 6.

White Jesus from Jesus of the Gospels, the one whose life, death, and resurrection demands sacrificial love as a response—a love ethic, to be sure—the kind the Prophet Isaiah instructs Hebrew people to follow in chapter 1, verse 17: learn to do good; seek justice, rescue the oppressed, defend the orphan, plead for the widow (NRSV).[77]

White Jesus and White privilege have benefited White people and those who have assimilated to Whiteness and dominance as a way of differentiating from their origins to achieve better living conditions. However, it has been very difficult for the majority culture in the U.S. to admit how they have advanced through this moral White agency even despite the evidence of all its injustices to people of color.[78]. The White Jesus construct has excluded many people from proper healthcare and educational access, marginalized people politically, criminalized black and brown bodies, and has continued to perpetuate oppression, violence, and subjugation.[79] The most dangerous aspect of White Jesus and White privilege is that it goes unacknowledged and unnamed.[80] As Jennifer Harvey stresses:

This concept [whiteness] can be difficult for whites to grasp deeply—in part because the language of reconciliation does not demand (or, in some ways, even allow) a specific discussion of "whiteness." Being challenged to think or talk about being "white" throws us into moral confusion and distress, in part because our experience of white racial hierarchy and privilege makes it possible for whites to let whiteness go unnoticed.[81]

This pervasive Whiteness began to take over Christianity after Constantine converted and made Christianity both acceptable and required in the fourth century. Although prior to this point darker images of Jesus were prevalent throughout the church, images of Jesus began to evolve to finally issue in the White Jesus with blue eyes that we have naively accepted as normative over the centuries.[82] White Jesus and White dominance can be seen on the campuses throughout the CCCU in the administration, faculty, and staff; but also, as a symbol "that is visible in paintings, photos, depictions, and mythologies surrounding the physical interpretation of the person of

77. Jun et al, White Jesus, xx.
78. Harvey, Dear White Christians, 156.
79. Harvey, Dear White Christians, 156.
80. Harvey, Dear White Christians, 134.
81. Harvey, Dear White Christians, 134.
82. Jun et al., White Jesus, xxi.

Jesus. There is a salient and underlying logic behind the symbol of a Jesus who looks Anglo Saxon."[83] We have already argued that race is a social construction, but it is equally true that White Jesus and his salvific powers are also socially constructed through White evangelical institutions.

White Jesus' political prowess showed in the 2016 election of the U.S. president. Alexander Jun et al. further claim that Trump won the election by an overwhelming "80% or 4 in 5 White evangelical voters."[84] They argue that this voting pattern follows the myth that to be truly Christian, one needs to be White, American, and Republican, while others argue similarly that CHE institutions in the CCCU usually ascribe to a predominantly White, male, conservative ethic.[85] As we have established, it is impossible to speak about the Christian faith in the U.S. without touching on the intersections of politics, economics, race, and power.

PROTESTANT HIGHER EDUCATION

Christian higher education (CHE) has its roots in Western Europe during the Middle Ages. By "meeting both cultural and ecclesiastical needs," these educational auxiliaries were primarily tied to the Roman Catholic Church, which prepared the way for the development of colleges and universities during the late twelfth and thirteenth centuries.[86] Hence, medieval universities were intentional about the integration of faith and learning, combating paganism and declaring that "all truth is God's truth."[87]

This concept of the university lasted throughout the Protestant Reformation, and although there were some differences between Catholic and Protestant curricula, most of the diversity was due to Christian humanism.[88] Harvard College (now University) was established by the New England Puritans in 1636, which gave birth to CHE in the U.S. However, the Revolutionary Period catapulted many innovations for CHE due to "America's cultural values [that] were in flux" which eventually gave birth to seminaries and theological schools.[89] Shortly after, Mark A. Noll explains:

---

83. Jun et al., White Jesus, 5.
84. Jun et al, White Jesus, 8.
85. Fubara et al, "Applying Diversity Management Principles," 119.
86. Patterson, Shining Lights, 16.
87. Patterson, Shining Lights, 16.
88. Patterson, Shining Lights, 16.
89. Ringenberg and Noll, The Christian College, 22.

The years from 1865 to 1900 constituted the great period of transition for American higher education. When Charles Eliot became president of Harvard in 1869, he set that influential institution on a course of innovation and expansion. The John Hopkins University, founded in 1876, exercised leadership in the establishment of graduate education. Other major changes were also under way: new universities were founded such as Cornell, Chicago, Stanford, and Clark; older private colleges such as Yale, Princeton, and Columbia were transformed into universities with the addition of graduate and professional schools; major state universities such as Michigan and Wisconsin grew up almost overnight in the Midwest and the West.[90]

Prior to the Revolution Period America experienced the Second Great Awakening which brought revival and inspired the birth of other colleges including Union University, Taylor University, and Wheaton College.[91] Interestingly, most schools in the Council of Christian Colleges and Universities (CCCU) trace their history to the evangelical renewal and revivalism of this time, principally from the Methodist and Baptist denominations.[92] John R. Thelin argues that by the time of the Revolutionary War colleges and their missions had drifted from religious underpinnings, as did their leadership, curriculum, and learning.[93] He does admit, however, that "religion occupied a central but confined place in the colonial colleges."[94]

After the Colonial Period, colleges like Harvard were searching for ways to reinvent themselves and remain culturally relevant. As Thelin states: "in both 1780 and 1980, academic leaders at the historic colleges realized that reliance on heritage without attention to the changing social and political environment was a blueprint for institutional erosion."[95] Said differently, sociocultural and socioeconomic trends inadvertently made institutions change their ways of conducting business and how they viewed the purpose of their existence.

Another view comes from William C. Ringenberg and Mark Noll: "with the exception of its numerical growth, higher education did not change dramatically between the Revolutionary and Civil War. Its dominantly intellectual force continued to be the Christian faith, and the curriculum changed

90. Ringenberg and Noll, The Christian College, 28.
91. Patterson, Shining Lights, 18.
92. Ringenberg and Noll, The Christian College, 57.
93. Thelin, History of American Higher Education, 28.
94. Thelin, History of American Higher Education, 13.
95. Thelin, History of American Higher Education, 40.

only modestly. Especially noteworthy, however, was the rise of the literary society as the primary extracurricular activity."[96] Despite diverse perspectives, however, one thing is certain: during these early years of university life campuses continued to evolve according to social shifts and demands. For example, shortly after the Civil War, American society began to go through several changes once again. According to James A. Patterson, pluralism undermined the dominant cultural Christianity with influences from newer immigrants that were Roman Catholic, Jewish, and Orthodox.[97] Science had also taken a more prominent seat, according to Patterson, related to Darwinian theory, a more socially conscious Christianity, and the dawn of the Industrial Revolution.[98] These trends began to shift the public opinion of CHE, to say the least.

THE BIRTH OF THE CCCU

Around the early 1900s, junior and teacher colleges began to sprout, especially in the West and throughout cities.[99] "By 1940, 11 percent of college students were enrolled in junior colleges, many of which were still attached to local high schools."[100] Nonsectarianism and secularization were not the only split occurring in higher education, but also under contestation was what distinguished an elite college or university from a junior school. One of the main differentiators among these models was determined by the type of students enrolled and the quality of undergraduate liberal education.[101]

During the end of the nineteenth and early twentieth centuries, colleges and universities commenced a process of nonsectarian secularization. Several reasons have been given for these shifts: (1) Patterson states that funding of such institutions in times of robust change was questionable, also noting the "declining appeal of a Christian worldview as the integrative center of educational pursuits";[102] (2) moral concerns shifted from the whole student to professionalism, civic duty, the rise of science, and the search for religious diversity,[103] and (3) social unrest was heightened, along with the

---

96. Ringenberg and Noll, The Christian College, 57.

97. Patterson, Shining Lights, 19.

98. Patterson, Shining Lights, 19.

99. Bastedo et al, American Higher Education, 22.

100. Bastedo et al, American Higher Education, 22.

101. Bastedo et al, American Higher Education, 23.

102. Patterson, Shining Lights, 20.

103. Glanzer et al, Restoring the Soul, 78.

demarcations of race, religion, and gender. However, Glanzer, Alleman and Ream stress:

> Of course, this fight was actually articulated as a fight for something more positive. American universities, both public and private, still sought first and foremost the unity of truth. They still wanted a soul—a common identity, story, and purpose. Yet after marginalizing theology they could not find an overarching narrative and structure that could embrace theological diversity or even a common vision of moral formation and inquiry. Consequently, the myth that excluding theology from the curriculum would bring a unity of objective knowledge to the university emerged. The fight against sectarian diversity would . . . be promulgated as an effort to emphasize Christian unity, but in the end it contributed to the secularization of the academy and the marginalization of moral education.[104]

During the Enlightenment era many institutions desired the separation of church and state, and this gave birth to many Bible colleges and other fundamentalist schools.[105] Nonetheless, by the 1950s evangelical educators were searching for a more unifying voice and movement to define Christian higher education (CHE), or to offer those who considered themselves "faith affirming." By 1971, more than eleven college presidents of CHE voted to make the Christian College Consortium (CCC) a reality.[106] The purpose of the CCC, according to Patterson, was:

> To promote the purposes of evangelical Christian higher education in the church and in society through the promotion of cooperation among evangelical colleges, and, in that conviction, to encourage and support scholarly research among Christian scholars for the purpose of integrating faith and learning; to initiate programs to improve the quality of instructional programs and encourage innovation in member institutions; to conduct research into the effectiveness of educational programs of the member colleges, with particular emphasis upon student development; to improve the management efficiency of the member institutions; to expand the human, financial and material resources available to the member institutions; to explore the feasibility of a university system of Christian colleges; and to do and perform all and everything which may be necessary and

---

104. Glanzer et al, Restoring the Soul, 79–80.
105. Yancey, Neither Jew nor Gentile, 27.
106. Patterson, Shining Lights, 27.

proper for the conduct of the activities of this organization in
the furtherance of the purposes heretofore expressed.[107]

One of the key tenets for the membership of the CCC was the integration of faith and learning, along with the desire to distinguish itself from fundamentalism.[108]

In 1976, the Christian College Coalition emerged and gave somewhat of an "umbrella" support system to the CCC. Through several changeovers at the presidential level, along with restructuring of the board of directors, another name change gave way to the Coalition of Christian Colleges and Universities. However, in a 1999 presidents' conference, a vote was held, and it was unanimously agreed to change the name one more time to the Council of Christian Colleges and Universities.[109] Today the CCCU is "a higher education association of more than 180 Christian institutions around the world,"[110] and considers itself the leading national voice of Christian higher education.[111]

CHE today lags behind public institutions in racial diversity on their campuses.[112] As stated by Fubara, Gardner, and Wolff: "Interestingly, Christian higher education institutions have struggled to keep up with the changes that have taken place in the larger society."[113] For some, changes in society enabled higher education to grow and expand its offerings to others. With the inclusion of African Americans after the *Brown v. Board of Education* decision in 1954 and then the Civil Rights movement in 1964, desegregation gained momentum and started the process of equity for marginalized communities to access education that was previously not afforded.[114] Today, higher education enrollment is "one-third minority . . . 13% Black, 12% Latino, 7% Asian American/Pacific Islander, 1% American Indian/Alaska Native."[115] Furthermore, by 2018, overall White student enrollment was 59%. In other words, higher education in the twenty-first century has continued to become more diverse racially and ethnically.

107. Patterson, Shining Lights, 32.

108. Patterson, Shining Lights, 33.

109. Patterson, Shining Lights, 93.

110. CCCU website, www.cccu.org.

111. CCCU website, www.cccu.org.

112. Yancey, Neither Jew nor Gentile, 28.

113. Fubara et al, "Applying Diversity Management Principles," 125.

114. Bastedo et al, American Higher Education, 25.

115. Bastedo et al, American Higher Education, 376.

In higher education, diversity, like technology, has become an impera-tive.[116] Changes from society and other factors have nudged CHE to move towards a more inclusive and diverse environment. But more work remains. As Daryl G. Smith suggests, "intentionality, rather than myths and excuses to explain a lack of progress, and fostering of synergy among the many cre-ative efforts and talented people already working in the area both appear to provide proactive and inclusive ways to create change."[117]

A succinct historical review of CHE has been offered, despite not giv-ing attention to key eras that merit their own chapters. There have been many changes and shifts that have caused strategic movements in the educa-tional enterprise, such as affirmative action, the GI Bill, the Enlightenment, the women's rights movement, the Morrill Act of 1862, the World Wars and other global phenomena. The next section of this chapter grapples with the DEI campus climate in the CCCU and how this pertains to Latinx and people of color overall.

THE CCCU'S DIVERSITY CAMPUS CLIMATE

Protestant schools historically have been more racially homogenous than other institutions of higher learning in the U.S.[118] Many evangelical institu-tions interpret a focus on diversity, equity, and inclusion as a symptom of secularization[119] And while racial diversity has become a regarded goal on college campuses,[120] CCCU schools have mostly taken aesthetic approaches to their diversity efforts, seldom challenging Whiteness and organizational performances[121] Said differently, safe conversations may take place on cam-pus, but looking deeply at policies, systems and structures, and traditions reveals that the embedded realities of white privilege and systemic racism continue to be addressed only on the surface, or worse, flat-out ignored.

CCCU schools are safe havens for White people. According to George Yancey, these White spaces include "characteristics such as individualism, color blindness, and Eurocentrism."[122] Institutions have worked hard at

---

116. Bastedo et al, American Higher Education, 397.

117. Quoted in Bastedo et al, American Higher Education, 397.

118. Yancey, Neither Jew nor Gentile, 3; Lang and Yandell, "Diversity Language as Systems Maintenance, 344; Fubara et al, "Applying Diversity Management Principles, 119.

119. Fubara et al, "Applying Diversity Management Principles, 118.

120. Yancey, Neither Jew nor Gentile, 6.

121. Lang and Yandell, "Diversity Language as Systems Maintenance," 344.

122. Yancey, Neither Jew nor Gentile, 9.

preserving a clan culture and spaces of exclusion. Furthermore, "people of color would find such institutions a bad fit for their own cultural, social, and political needs."[123] As Fubara, Gardner and Wolff assert:

> Interestingly, Christian higher education institutions have struggled to keep up with the changes that have taken place in the larger society. In spite of the value that these institutions ascribe to unconditional love and acceptance, they struggle to adopt a culture that is welcoming to people, even fellow Christians, from diverse backgrounds. Clearly, these institutions face a certain tension between embracing and rejecting diversity.[124]

However, people of color, and Latinx in particular, continue to enroll, seeking to find a quality Christian education that is based on Christian treatment and values.

Although many think the myth is true that diversity secularizes campuses, on the contrary, Kristin Paredes-Collins argues that students of color come to the campuses with a higher spiritual standard than their White counterparts, often leaving them with a void.[125] And although CCCU schools pride themselves on spiritually developing their students, the exclusion of "others" in the community hinders the spiritual growth of both White students and students of color. Consequently, in addition to Christian colleges failing to provide the best academic experience for students of color[126] they also fall short in developing both White students and students of color in their faith.[127]

The main differentiator between Christian colleges (the CCCU) and secular colleges is the obvious integration of faith in curriculum and the community. Students come to the CCCU with the desire to develop and mature in their faith walk, yet many are confronted with a gospelized Whiteness that leaves them excluded unless they assimilate. According to Paredes-Collins, "evangelical institutions intentionally promote spiritual growth and development but are lacking in the ability to provide a climate that enhances the spirituality of students from diverse backgrounds."[128] Paredes-Collins further declares that CCCU schools can address this equity issue by creating an environment characterized in the following ways:

123. Yancey, Neither Jew nor Gentile, 10.

124. Fubara et al, "Applying Diversity Management Principles," 125.

125. Paredes-Collins, "Cultivating Diversity and Spirituality," 126.

126. Yancey, Neither Jew nor Gentile, 28–29.

127. Yancy's work is comprehensive and is complemented by the participant narratives later in this book.

128. Paredes-Collins, "Cultivating Diversity and Spirituality," 135.

"(a) Sense of belonging is crucial to the faith development of students of color, (b) positive cross-racial interactions and compositional diversity are essential to a positive climate for diversity, and (c) the religious and societal norms established by the White majority need to be examined because of increasing demographic diversity."[129]

Besides the chapels and campus climates expressing Whiteness throughout the fabric of culture, students of color must deal with many institutional barriers.[130] Several of these barriers include the following challenges: (1) the majority of faculty, staff and administration are White; (2) many times students are seen as the representative for their culture (ethnic community), (3) students experience fatigue for having to "fight the current" much of the time; and (4) their cultural norms are excluded. It seems that CCCU schools must address their Eurocentric ideologies to better address their diversity pursuits—or their lack thereof.[131]

Diversifying campuses does not start with students, however. It starts at the top of the institution's leadership ranks. According to Kathleen Nussbaum and Heewon Chang, "Building board capacity is critical for Christian higher education institutions to effectively embrace diversity as an integral part of their institutional mission, values and ethos, and commitment to justice."[132] The authors add that a diverse pipeline of administrators of color is also needed to move the diversity agenda further along in CHE. Their argument rests on the fact that despite efforts in the last few decades, "racial, ethnic, and gender disparities continue to persist in higher education."[133] Some of the main issues they articulate for consideration are that the majority of tenured faculty are not people of color, women continue to be rare or absent at the highest ranks of leadership, and worst, theological justifications are given to validate these inequities.[134] Nussbaum and Chang maintain that the same theological foundations should be utilized to create sustained diversity within campuses by expressing the multifold expressions of God.[135] It seems that the intersection of the mission and vision of a campus, administrative leadership, board capacity, and diverse faculty could enable a CCCU school to move in the right direction.

129. Paredes-Collins, "Cultivating Diversity and Spirituality," 131.
130. Yancey, Neither Jew nor Gentile, 19.
131. Paredes-Collins, "Cultivating Diversity and Spirituality," 129.
132. Nussbaum and Chang, Quest for Diversity, 5.
133. Nussbaum and Chang, Quest for Diversity, 6.
134. Nussbaum and Chang, Quest for Diversity, 6.
135. Nussbaum and Chang, Quest for Diversity, 7.

Joel Pérez conducted interviews and analyzed data across four CCCU schools and found that besides board capacity, executive leadership and faculty support, diversity efforts were sustained by the schools' biblical mandate and their institutional mission.[136] When it comes to institutional diversity efforts, Pérez explains:

> Schools should start their efforts by analyzing their mission to evaluate whether they are truly committed to trying to make progress, and officially stating the theology behind these efforts . . . If the institution is not going to start with these efforts, it should abandon them, for if they do not view diversity as part of their mission, their efforts can only be moderately successful at best.[137]

George Yancy found that Protestant schools prefer to downplay diversity issues and even pretend that systemic racism doesn't exist on campuses.[138] A key identifier of this type of individualist culture in CCCU schools is an insistence on "colorblindness," which functions as an effective barrier to grappling with racial issues because they do not exist in the first place.[139] The result is that these types of institutions create atmospheres that are less favorable to people of color; therefore, they only need to address concerns that can be narrated as isolated events, not as the systemic and cultural problems of inclusion and racial discrimination that they are.

The Whiteness that pervades CHE, undermining any view of systemic racism on campus, creates a new set of problems, including the communication that takes place surrounding diversity agendas. According to Justin Lang and Lonnie Yandell, "diversity language functions to conceal operations of systemic racism on campuses, producing inaction and/or 'cosmetic' action that does not threaten whiteness as a position of privilege and power. White racial comfort goes unchallenged, with White students, faculty, and staff not having to recognize their complicity in campus racism or engage with racism themselves."[140] The question then becomes, if you don't think there is a problem and that everything is just fine, why would you entertain a discussion, much less think that anything needs to change? The result is usually that nothing changes, and conversations generally uphold the status quo of the institution and its organizational frameworks.

---

136. Pérez, "Diversity at Christian Colleges," 27.
137. Pérez, "Diversity at Christian Colleges," 32.
138. Yancey, Neither Jew nor Gentile, 25.
139. Yancey, Neither Jew nor Gentile, 25.
140. Lang and Yandell, "Diversity Language as Systems Maintenance," 343.

Lang and Yandell found that diversity language in CCCU schools is used as a public relations scheme that seems progressive and demonstrates sensitivity but really doesn't challenge the inequities of the systems, structures and policies that are in place.[141] This language is thus *nonperformative*, meaning it does not produce what it claims to achieve. Lang and Yandell describe this nonperformative diversity language in three stages: (a) commitment to diversity, (b) celebrate diversity, and (c) diversity as public relations.[142] The authors explain that a commitment to diversity basically means that statements and documents are formulated as trophies, but the institution never gets around to doing the actual diversity work that shifts the culture. Celebrating diversity simply means focusing on differences in culture by eating food and celebrating certain days and months of the year, but never getting to the differences of power, equity, privilege, and the everyday struggle for people of color.[143] And while diversity in the public relations schema is presented as an important value, action is never taken to make greater diversity a reality. It is basically a promotional or marketing tool that showcases examples of diversity as tokens but never gets around to committing to the work of equal respect, love and justice.

Racism and discrimination have permeated CHE since its inception, demonstrated by the fact that black students did not have access to these Christian institutions until the middle of the twentieth century.[144] Theological foundations, political associations and geographical locations all have a history, defining institutions and institutional responses as changes in society were occurring in the U.S. prior to, during, and after the Civil Rights movement. As Anthea Butler explains:

> When Evangelicals married their educational and religious institutions to nationalism and political power starting in the 1950's, they gained a foothold that has now become a stronghold. Evangelicals became well educated, and they shaped their historical narrative more around theology and esoteric boundaries, mostly white cultural boundaries, ignoring their social and historical connections to broader American life. Each succeeding decade, they embraced more political power. By 2016, they were willing to embrace a man devoid of the morality evangelicals have preached about, written about, and enforced,

141. Lang and Yandell, "Diversity Language as Systems Maintenance," 344.
142. Lang and Yandell, "Diversity Language as Systems Maintenance," 346.
143. Lang and Yandell, "Diversity Language as Systems Maintenance," 346.
144. Jun et al., White Jesus, 74.

in order to retain it. Trump isn't the reason why evangelicals turned to racism. They were racist all along.[145]

These aspects of discrimination will need to be addressed if CHE desires to move towards a racially just and inclusive campus environment.

FINAL THOUGHTS

God has used Christian higher education (CHE) to transform my own life through the development of my thinking and leadership practice. Jesus once declared, "Love the Lord your God with all your heart and with all your soul and with all your strength and with all your mind" (Luke 10:27, NIV). While growing up, my faith tradition never emphasized the "thinking" part of our relationship with Jesus, but definitely taught the "heart, soul, and strength" of this pericope. My encounter with CHE allowed me to experience religion in a new way, providing me with greater tools for the ministry to which I have been called. The CCCU affirms its Christian mission as:

> Committed to supporting, protecting, and promoting the value of integrating the Bible—divinely inspired, true, and authoritative—throughout all curricular and co-curricular aspects of the educational experience on our campuses, including teaching and research. We support a coherent approach to education in which the development of the mind, spirit, body, and emotions are seamlessly woven together in the quest not just for knowledge but also for wisdom.[146]

CHE occupies a unique space in society, but especially vis-a-vis the church. While there exist in the U.S. more than 1,024 religious affiliated institutions, currently the CCCU has 144 institutions (CCCU website). The CCCU is differentiated from other religiously affiliated schools because of its faith integration throughout the curriculum. "The CCCU's mission is to advance the cause of Christ-centered higher education and to help [its] institutions transform lives by faithfully relating scholarship and service to biblical truth." In other words, the CCCU is dedicated to serving Christian students, who in turn serve the church and the world.

The CCCU can be considered a consortium (consisting of 180 institutions) that are in alignment with the mission of God. As Douglas McConnell proclaims:

---

145. Butler, White Evangelical Racism, 141.
146. Council for Christian Colleges and Universities, "About Our Work and Mission."

> [I] applied the concept of missional to organizations with an
> orientation toward the mission of God in order to make it clear
> that such an organization is defined by its purposes to serve God
> through its practices and products. This includes a wide range
> of Christian organizations, large and small, high profile and
> low profile, but always characterized by their commitment to
> serving God. An organization committed to serving God must
> continually ensure that its practices and products are honoring
> to God. Thus, to think missiologically about organizations is to
> consider their significant contributions, in all that they are and
> do, in relation to the mission of God.[147]

To avoid confusion, I would like to clarify what I mean by "mission of God" versus an organizational mission that may align with the *Missio Dei*. The mission of God (or the *Missio Dei*) starts with the Holy Trinity and signifies the redemption of the world.[148] The Christian church is called and invited by God to participate in mission by collaborating with the Holy Spirit for the liberation and salvation of individuals, nations, and cultures. As Samuel Escobar declared, the heart of Christian mission is "the drive to share the good news with all, to cross every border with the gospel."[149] The CCCU has joined the church in her mission to align with the *Missio Dei* by educating and equipping her for the work of the ministry (Eph. 4:11–13). The CCCU is thinking missiologically about her service to the church and the broader mission of God. Therefore, I have a burden to see the CCCU address its diversity efforts holistically and with greater commitment and intentionality. The church in the U.S. and globally is continuing to become more female, black and brown. If the CCCU does not align with this reality it could possibly see extinction.

I once heard a pastor proclaim that "the church was the hope of the world." But if the church is divided, how can she bring a liberative message if she is too busy destroying herself? Jesus said that a house divided against itself cannot stand (Matt 12:22–28). Can the church and Christian higher education (CHE) stand in the twenty-first century against evil and sin in the world? The bride of Christ has the word of God to stand on as an eternal rock. Jesus said that the "gates of hell could not prevail" against her (Matt 16:17–19).

Unity for the U.S. evangelical church in the twenty-first century will need to be her priority. The mission of Christ on earth can no longer be

147. McConnell, Cultural Insights for Christian Leaders, 21–22.

148. McConnell, Cultural Insights for Christian Leaders, 2.

149. Escobar, New Global Mission, 13.

hindered in the West because of the divisive racist spirit that pervades her. About 90 percent of Americans who state that they are evangelicals are White.[150] Most of these Christians voted for Trump, a person who has made sexist and racist remarks without apology. This segment of the church would benefit from learning from its multicultural counterparts and submitting to a transformational process. Historically, the White evangelical church has done more to propagate a racialized society than it has to diminish it.[151] Additionally, although white evangelicals proclaim that we live in a post racial society, those who live within the margins know too well that systemic bigotry still chokes the life of the church in the U.S. Correspondingly, there is a need for repentance, forgiveness, reparations, and reconciliation.[152] The issue remains that the White evangelical church has desired to quickly receive forgiveness and reconciliation, without reparation and repentance.

Unity for the U.S. evangelical church will not come overnight and ignoring the facts about systemic racism and institutional division will not make these realities go away.[153] This work of unity through diversity will take work, cultural responsiveness, and humility. "White evangelical Protestants are accountable freewill individualists. Unlike progressives, for them individuals exist independent of structures and institutions, have freewill, and are individually accountable for their own actions."[154] In other words, to move forward in unity, the White evangelical church will have to deconstruct her individualistic views that assume that people can be understood separately from societal structures and systems. White evangelicals will have to recognize that context affects everyone.

The White Jesus will have to be put away by evangelicals in the U.S. This Christ exemplar promotes unequal power, and economic advantage for the majority culture, as well as injustices done to the poor. As James H. Cone states: "the white Christ gave blacks slavery, segregation, and lynching and told them to turn the other cheek and to look for their reward in heaven. Be patient, they were told, and your suffering will be rewarded, for it is the source of your spiritual redemption."[155] The Christ that the U.S. evangelical church will have to accept as their "personal and public savior" will be Latinx, Asian, African, Black, Brown, and bicultural (and possibly female!).

---

150. Emerson and Smith, Divided by Faith, 3.

151. Emerson and Smith, Divided by Faith, 170.

152. Harvey, Dear White Christians, 189–190.

153. Emerson and Smith, Divided by Faith, 82.

154. Emerson and Smith, Divided by Faith, 76.

155. Cone, Cross and Lynching Tree, 119.

Expressions of biblical justice must be the work of the evangelical church in the U.S. Concepts of "justice" can no longer be dismissed as "just social justice" or a "liberal agenda," but must be embraced as the justice of God that allows the church to "act justly and to love mercy and to walk humbly with [their] God" (Mic 6:8, NIV). This justice will flow from the ghettoes to the suburbs, from the ivory tower to public housing, and from the White House to Latin America. This type of justice will bring liberation for all people economically, politically, educationally, religiously, and socially. This calls the church to a mutual suffering and rejoicing, as Cone affirmed:

> But we cannot find liberating joy in the cross by spiritualizing it, by taking away its message of justice in the midst of powerlessness, suffering, and death. The cross, as a locus of divine revelation, is not good news for the powerful, for those who are comfortable with the way things are, or for anyone whose understanding of religion is aligned with power. The religious authorities of Jesus' time were threatened by his teachings about the reign of God's justice and love, and the state authorities executed him as an insurrectionist—one who "perverts the nation" and "stirs up the people" (Luke 23:2, 5).[156]

In 2017, Fuller Theological Seminary's School of Intercultural Studies (now the School of Mission and Theology) hosted a conference that produced a book called *Can "White" People be Saved?*, edited by Love Sechrest, Johnny Ramírez-Johnson, and Amos Yong. This startling title generated attention. Can White people be saved? Of course they can, and many are. It is hard to believe anything else in the West, since it has been assumed that if a person is White, they are Christian, or at least the right type of Christian. But this "fusion" of Whiteness and Christian identity, as Willie J. Jennings calls it,[157] is what I have been challenging in this chapter. We have assumed Whiteness to be normative in the U.S. due to the influence of the American historical colonial project, and this normalcy has produced a hatred in the U.S. for anything that challenges the majority of conservative White, Republican, male-dominant, evangelical Protestants. Nevertheless, many have ignored the fact that this wedding of faith with White privilege is part of the bigger problem. As Jennings states:

> It is precisely this fusing together of Christianity with whiteness that constitutes the ground for many of our struggles today. The

---

156. Cone, Cross and Lynching Tree, 156.

157. Quoted in Sechrest et al, Can "White" People be Saved?, 28.

struggle against aggressive nationalism is the struggle against the fusion of Christianity and whiteness. The struggle against racism and white supremacy and some aspects of sexism and patriarchy is the struggle against this fusion. The struggle against the exploitation of the planet is bound up in the struggle against this joining. So many people today see these problems— of planetary exploitation, of racism, of sexism, of nationalism, and so forth—but they do not see the deeper problem of this fusion, which means they have not yet grasped the energy that drives many of our problems.[158]

It will be a very difficult task for White Christians to give up power, share brain space, and open doors for others to participate and contribute. However, if the church and CHE in the U.S. would like to make a broader impact within the U.S. and abroad, these colonial associations of the evangelical faith will have to be dismantled. The church moving forward in mission for the twenty-first century will have to do as Jesus did; dying for neighbors and committing herself to the ones for whom Jesus died—the poor, the lost, and the "least of these."[159] The problem in society is not so much a social justice issue, but a problem that the church and CHE must address as biblical justice.[160]

158. Quoted in Sechrest et al, Can "White" People be Saved?, 28.

159. Costas, Christ Outside the Gate, 190–191.

160. Costas, Christ Outside the Gate, 190.

4

Testimonios[1]

> As the Latinx/a/o community makes sense of our stories, our ideas are (re)braided, creating generations of difference and similarity that are woven together to tell our stories as well as those of our parents and grandparents. These blended stories draw on experience as a source of strength, which we use as we navigate institutions of higher education that were not necessarily built with people of color in mind.[2]

Research on people of color in Christian Higher Education (CHE) is limited.[3] One of the main impetuses for this research project has been an attempt to fill that void. I set out to understand the experiences of executive Latinx leaders in the CCCU, with the hopes of creating a foundation for future research. In U.S. higher education overall, "only sixteen percent of all senior administrators are people of color,"[4] Latinas make up 5.1 percent of the executive ranks, compromise 4.7 percent of the professional ranks, and 10.6 percent of the nonprofessional ranks in higher education.[5] Moffit

---

1. Testimonios (testimonies); I am using the Spanish word to refer to the narratives, experiences, and stories of the executive Latinx leaders in Christian higher education, thereby, again, seeking to provide Christian legitimacy to CRT and LatCrit methods as Christian testimonies.

2. Batista et al, Latinx/a/os in Higher Education, ixx.

3. Longman, Diversity Matters, 33.

4. León and Martinez, Latino College Presidents, 270.

5. León and Martinez, Latino College Presidents, 2.

found that there were twice the number of administrators of color serving at nonreligious institutions of higher learning than those serving at religiously affiliated institutions.[6] In other words, public higher education institutions are more diverse than religious higher education institutions in their leadership.

Diversifying the leadership pipeline in the CCCU has been complicated, to say the least. Pete Menjares asked the question:

> [A]re faith-based schools ready to have the difficult conversations on race, white privilege, the prevalence of white cultural norms, and other systemic barriers that limit the inclusion of diverse leadership and impede genuine progress toward racial solidarity? Regardless of how one answers these questions, the educational institution of the future will be diverse, and we must remain intentional about developing the next generation of leaders who visibly and culturally reflect the depth and breadth of the kingdom of God.[7]

This chapter sets out to accomplish one thing: to give voice to those who historically have been minoritized and marginalized in CHE. Critical Race (CRT) and LatCrit Theory, along with Narrative Inquiry and Intersectionality are used to chronicle interviewees' experiences and stories within the CCCU and throughout their higher education journey. While research is nonexistent on executive Latinx leaders in the CCCU, this project will serve as a starting point for future research to be conducted.

EXPERIENCES OF EXECUTIVE LATINX LEADERS

The executive Latinx leaders selected to participate in this project all held a rank of dean or above (that is, dean, vice president, provost, and so forth)[8] and were serving in a member or affiliate member school of the CCCU. All interviewees held PhD degrees and were from Latina family origin. Most held faculty roles before becoming administrators, and some still teach. All their names are concealed for identity purposes, due to the limited presence of potential interviewees in the CCCU, and I have omitted anything that could clearly reveal their identity to readers. On the other hand, information disclosed in Table One is provided with the participants' permission. Three interviewees were female and two were male, and the names given to

---

6. Longman, Diversity Matters, 127.

7. Longman, Diversity Matters, 25.

8. All Latinx will be referred to as participants or interviewees from here on out.

them are: Marisol, Ruth, Yanisa, Tomás and Josue.[9] Race and ethnicity represented were Mexican American, Dominican, Puerto Rican, and Cuban, and all consider themselves Latina or Latino. Please refer to Table One for more details of the Latinx leaders interviewed.

TABLE 1: LATINX LEADERS INTERVIEWED

Participant	Highest degree obtained	Total years in HE/CHE	Born in US?	Parents born in US?	Ethnicity
Yanisa	PhD	30	Yes	Yes	Mexican American
Josue	PhD	31	Yes	Mother Yes Father No	Latino
Marisol	PhD	30	Yes	Yes	Puerto Rican
Ruth	PhD	19	Yes	Yes	Puerto Rican
Tomás	PhD	18	No	No	Latino

Today's college students are more diverse than ever before in the history of U.S. higher education,[10] and Christian higher education (CHE) is not immune from this demographic trend. Research suggests that in order to serve this diverse student population, traditional faculty, staff and administration roles need to be reframed to serve more broadly; for example, as "teacher, tutor, mentor, and counselor."[11] A unique contribution that leaders of color and Latinx in particular bring to the table is the ability to engage students of color and provide mentorship. The intersectionality of identities that this new student body brings to the CCCU is well matched with the intersectionality of the multiple worlds Latinx leaders have had to navigate, not only in their lives, but in their higher education journey.

According to the interviewees, leading and serving in the CCCU is very difficult, to say the least. Not only do these leaders have the task of working twice as hard to be taken seriously, but they also have the blessed burden of being a mentor to underserved students and other leaders of color.[12] All interviewees described their experience as a true blessing, but they

9. All interviews were conducted in confidentiality, and the names of interviewees are withheld by mutual agreement.

10. Conrad and Gasman, Educating a Diverse Nation, 257.

11. Conrad and Gasman, Educating a Diverse Nation, 270.

12. Marisol, Ruth, Yanisa, Tomás, Josue.

also stated that the work can be very consuming, tiresome, and laborious. In other words, they go above and beyond the call of duty.[13] Latinx leaders in higher education have less room for error than their White counterparts and feel that they are continuously under scrutiny,[14] but this drives them to have a strong work ethic.[15]

The experiences of Latinas in the CCCU are as diverse as the leaders themselves. Tomás explained that his experience has been "hard, challenging, and rewarding." According to Tomás, the notion of working twice as hard to be considered half as good matches his lived experience. Tomás further declared that it was difficult to be himself, or to be, in other words "Latino." According to Tomás, many microaggressions are expressed towards Latinx leaders in CHE. Instead of expertise and leadership being celebrated, many times such expertise and leadership is treated as suspect by the majority culture.[16]

All interviewees expressed their frustrations and described numerous direct experiences with discrimination and bias on campus. Latinx leaders expressed the reality of structural issues at their universities and how these issues were barriers to their personal growth and sense of inclusion. Although most CCCU schools assert that they desire diversity, according to the Latinx leaders interviewed, most campuses are not conducive to or supportive of diverse leadership and minoritized students. Change is necessary for the progress of both population groups within CHE.

SYSTEMIC RACISM EXPERIENCED BY LATINX

Systemic racism is alive and well within the CCCU. The participants in this research project all disclosed experiencing systemic racism and facing issues with prejudice, and conveyed feeling discriminated against—from microaggressions to the double standards that they witnessed within the systems, policies and structures of their institutions.

CCCU schools were not created with people of color in mind. Nonetheless, diverse leadership is crucial for building institutional capacity for diversity, equity and inclusion.[17] It seems counterintuitive for institutions to declare that they want diversity, yet to do everything in their power to prohibit growth in this area. This was an irritation that all interviewees

13. Núñez et al, Hispanic-Serving Institutions, 148.

14. León and Martinez, Latino College Presidents, 272.

15. Tomás, Marisol, Ruth, Yanisa, Josue.

16. Tomás.

17. Smith, Diversity's Promise, 147.

voiced and lived. Tomás, in particular, offered several profound testimonies to his experiences with discrimination in CHE. When asked, he declared:

> What have I encountered? . . . Direct oppression by board members second-guessing [me], lack of support by the president . . . I find oftentimes the sense of: "we're giving you a pass." I think that the byproduct effect of affirmative action policies where we still have some of these questioning whether or not you really have made it and whether or not you really belong. Those are kinds of things that happen quite often . . . we also have the microaggression issues that are always present, like, "Oh, you're the senior vice president? Nice to meet you," rather than "nice to meet you, sir," you know . . . there's a sense of confidence that you believe that someone like me could actually be in a senior vice president position. But I oftentimes find people being surprised that I hold such title . . . rather than affirming.
>
> There are still some structural issues in Christian higher education . . . there is some elements of obstruction of justice that's manifested in Christian higher education . . . especially if you align yourself for the students. If, as a leader with a Latino background like I am, aligned myself with students you automatically get a target on you if you will, in terms of "what are you trying to do" type questions . . . Expected stereotypes oftentimes are alluded to and the breaking of those stereotypes then creates the: "Oh, I guess you're not Latin after all . . . " I mean those are subtle but they are there and more structural in some cases particularly when those with power above . . . The incidents of board members trying to force their power on you are a little bit more prevalent . . . At least I find that particularly in my experience.[18]

There was a sense of disappointment from Tomás since he had served in CHE eighteen years and felt that he had always tried to prove himself. The lack of support, even in his position as an executive leader, was disappointing, to say the least. According to Tomás, being oppressed by board members as a Latinx was all too common. Instead of being accepted and affirmed, he felt rejected and marginalized.

Participants were in agreement that there are serious structural issues within the CCCU that privilege some while excluding others. According to Ruth, the CHE system is broken: "there is institutional racism." She further acknowledged:

18. Tomás.

Needless to say . . . there's a danger to being oppressed for such a long time that you live into the oppression. *Los Israelitas* [the Israelites], the people of God prayed, prayed, and prayed. God, take us out of Egypt there's a new Pharaoh in town . . . it's hard work, take us out of here! God takes them out and they have the opportunity to go down a pathway that is shorter than the route they end up going, but God has to make the decision of keeping them in that route because he is afraid they will go back to the same oppression that they asked to release them from. So there's this danger of living the oppressed life for such a long time that you live into the victimization of it. And by your actions or by your silence, even though you have been silenced, you grow comfortable in that silence and contribute to that colonialist mindset that continues to have the systems bound and the people bound.[19]

Ruth explained that Latinx and people of color in CHE have been oppressed and ostracized for so long that they have grown comfortable with it, or at least, it has become normalized. The fight for justice and equality for many seems to get snuffed out. The systems within CHE have Latinx bound to minimal influence and leadership potential, to the point where becoming an executive leader is somewhat of a miracle in itself. Ruth asserted that this was primarily due to the lack of accountability with the broader system:

There is a huge lack to be able to hold accountable and to have institutions to serve in the role of advocacy. To help institutions that are bound by the stronghold of institutional racism; for their inability to make the shift of fully understanding diversity and creating the pathways of a diverse body. There is a lot of things that I would like to do, but there is nobody holding anyone accountable in this area. And diverse candidates, who is training them and creating a pipeline? There is a deficiency in that area.

And who is asking the institutions to create the pipeline and equipping them to make sure that they are diverse? We have been talking about the pockets forever in terms of faculty representation and the diversity there; in terms of student population and the diversity there; in terms of administration even at the level of presidents. There are huge gaps that exist. We have taken steps towards the right direction, but at the pace that we are going, are we really going to experience it?[20]

19. Ruth.
20. Ruth.

Participants shared frustration with the lack of intentionality by the CCCU and their institutions. Said differently, they felt that there was no sense of urgency when it came to diversifying administration and faculty. Although there is much talk, although many task force and committee meetings are held, when it came to committing to concretely change the organizational culture and structure that continue to preserve systemic racism, there was literally no movement. Ruth's question in the previous quote is telling and worth restating: "We have taken steps towards the right direction, but at the pace that we are going, are we really going to experience [change]?"

Systemic Racism and Current Events

At the time of this writing (2020–21), there has been much racial tension and unrest in the U.S. due to police brutality. The country watched in horror as George Floyd, an African American, was murdered in the streets of Minnesota in broad daylight by a white police officer pinning him down to the ground with his knee on his neck for more than eight minutes. Breonna Taylor, a 26-year-old African American emergency medical technician, was shot in Louisville, Kentucky in her own apartment by three white police officers. In yet another recent incident, Jacob Blake was shot seven times in the back, in front of his three children who were in the car. These are not the first, and sadly, they will not be the last racist incidents that we will experience as American citizens. However, what has made the impact unique in this time are the videos that were captured live by citizens who just happened to be present.

I asked all the participants in this project to share their thoughts about these events and to reflect on how they related to Christian higher education (CHE). Yanisa asserted:

> I think what was so tragic about George Floyd is, well think about it . . . people say I don't know what systemic racism is . . . well let me tell you what that is . . . One, the cop did what he did and the other cops backed him up, so there's this culture of whatever they say goes . . . then you notice that the coroner says he [George Floyd] must've had preexisting conditions and he may have been on drugs. So that coroner is part of that systemic racism. Not only do you have the police, then you have the coroner, and then the district attorney, if we would have allowed that, he would have said there's no charges because they were reasonable within their rights or whatever . . . so systemic

racism is . . . one system that backs up another system that backs up another system within a unit.

I explain that to my people and say look, you know, we may hire at the entrance but then your culture in your department is that you push people down to fit into a certain mold. If they don't fit in that mold then we punish them by giving them really bad assignments and so then we participate in that . . . or our personnel committee doesn't promote them or tenure them because they don't fit into a mold that we say exists . . . even though the rest of the world doesn't understand that system because we're not a scholarship place, we are about teaching and yet we punish them when it comes to scholarship at the personnel committee. And then the board of trustees backs that up, then the provost and the president say, "well that's what the personnel committee said so that's how it goes." So that's what systemic racism looks like. For me, systemic racism is one system that supports another system to keep things in a certain way. And if you had those systems break apart and begin to change then it weakens the whole structure, and that's what we need to focus on. That's what I'm focusing on.[21]

Yanisa was adamant about the ways in which systemic racism is interwoven in the fabric of U.S. society and how it replicates itself smoothly in CHE. The fact that a police officer could kill a black man in plain daylight with other cops by his side, and that the officers would not do anything for over eight minutes even while George Floyd was begging to be let up because he could not breathe, speaks to the reality of people of color in the U.S. Yanisa described this reality in CHE in terms of one unit backing up another unit, then it gets backed up by others in support of their bias and prejudice towards Latinx and other people of color. In other words, the system in CHE allows for discrimination against Latinx in a similar way to which the U.S. police system allows for the dehumanization of black and brown people. The interviewees expressed their fatigue with these racist incidents and their work in CHE.

Participants commented on systemic racism in society and CHE as something that was common knowledge, contrary to some popular opinion that the U.S. is a post-racialized society. We see this myth promulgated in various places. Kimberly Guilfoyle stated in the 2020 Republican National Convention that racism did not exist in America and that the best was yet to come. She also mentioned that she was a first-generation American, which

21. Yanisa.

is misleading since all Puerto Ricans are American citizens due to the Island's territory status as a commonwealth of the United States.

Ruth, who is Puerto Rican, seemed to think differently than Guilfoyle. She stressed that CHE and the church needed to do a better job at addressing racism.

> So systemic racism now is not with a question mark. . .now, everybody knows systemic racism exists, and now the question is what do we do about it? I do feel that even the experience that I was in has to some degree helped me to be able to engage in conversations that I probably would have never been a part of because I am a victim of systemic racism. I have experienced the clause of systemic racism and having done so then it brings me to a place where now I am interested in contributing to the transformation of institutions because they have to deal with the systemic racism in order for them to not only thrive.
>
> Yes, I get the importance that financial sustainability is thriving . . . but we are talking about the Kingdom of God and there's just no way to work around that as Christian higher education. And when the NBA and other secular institutions are doing this better than the church then, hello—hello! It's time for us to really take a second look and have a "come to Jesus" meeting with ourselves so that there's changes that happen within us and we embody who we've been entrusted to be—the body of Christ.[22]

Ruth mentioned that secular institutions like the National Basketball Association (NBA) have taken concrete steps to address social disparities and issues of racism, while on the other hand CHE and churches seem to be silent. The participants all stated that silence was not an option in these times. In other words, if you are silent than you are complicit with the injustices that are transpiring.

Tomás named divisive leadership at the national level as an important factor fueling the racist incidents we are experiencing.

> We still have leadership in place at the political level that throws gasoline into fire regardless of political bent. Someone whose rhetoric is not of unifying language, rather very much more divisive . . .so I think that plays a part into it. I think since then we've gotten from Charlottesville all the way up to now . . . think about the last three years . . . the last three years has been an accumulation of dormant issues.[23]

22. Ruth.
23. Tomás.

Tomás was under the impression that the last three years of national political leadership have been promulgating division and racism. He mentioned that under the previous president there was an accumulation of tension and racist undertones; therefore, this has created fuel for social unrest. None of the interviewees stated anything positive about Donald Trump in terms of unifying the people. Instead, they believed that he was one of the main reasons that so much White supremacy was being manifested.

Josue added that justice could no longer be something to wait for. He mentioned that the time for diversity for CHE was now.

> I do believe that I've said this publicly . . . the George Floyd moment for our nation is a watershed moment. We have entered a new era from my perspective and can't go back. So I want to say . . . as a result of that occurrence and the way the world responded, which from my perspective is generally appropriate . . . I think it is reflective of something deeply spiritual at some level and it is incumbent upon leaders of color in particular, to step up to say that there may have been a tolerance for waiting even if it were for another year or two; that is done, we're done with that now. So I would say the urgency that I think you heard from me even two years ago, now has come to a new level and I think we have to demand more, we must demand more of everyone in higher education; but in particular this idea of how do we help ensure that there are diverse voices at the highest levels and opportunities at those levels as well, and that we are the ones who are helping to shape the conversation . . .[24]

For Josue, the protests witnessed in the streets since May 2020 are "deeply spiritual." None of the participants supported looting or rioting, but they were all in support of peaceful protests and demonstrations. Change rarely has taken place in the U.S. without protests, so it was not surprising for these Latinx leaders to state that they thought God was in this movement and that CHE must choose to be a part of this historic time of justice if it truly desires diversity.

Racism and discrimination do not occur only from a monoculture group towards others. According to the participants, Latinas are totally against racism or any discriminatory experience. However, Ruth mentioned that Latinas often express discriminatory behavior toward each other, depending on our skin pigmentation. "*Mi gente primero* [my people first]," declared Ruth. But Ruth further stated that we are to use our cultures to reconcile the cultures of the world to God, and not to divide ourselves. If we

24. Josue.

behave favorably towards one another, "the missiological table gets bigger."[25] According to Ruth, true reconciliation can only be accomplished when we first reconcile with God. This in turn, creates the conditions for us to love one another.

Josue expressed isolation in his role as a leader within the Hispanic community. Although there is philosophical support existent in CHE, this support does not seem to manifest in practical ways. All of the interviewees spoke of institutional bias and the fact that the CCCU is not ready for Latinx leaders. Although many of these institutions desire more Latinx students, Josue mentioned that budget constraints do not allow for diversifying strategies to address the needs of this unique population. Josue described the lack of mentorship for Latinas as another issue for institutions, as well as Latinx being nonexistent in board leadership. This all creates a lack of exposure for young Latina leaders in CHE. Josue stated:

> I think I have been very privileged not to face other barriers that other Latinx leaders have. As awful as it sounds just speaking in stark reality; the fact that I did not inherit my father's dark skin color worked in my favor, especially earlier on in my career. But I think that the inherent barrier of darker skin people have experienced for centuries in this white-dominated society is something that I never faced because I do not look like a Hispanic.[26]

It is interesting to note that although Josue does not think he looks Latino, this has not protected him from experiencing some prejudice and bias because of his last name. He stated, "it was a little isolating for me as a leader within the Hispanic community and I did not sense in CHE a clear commitment to Latino leaders. I think it took some time to get the conversation going." For Josue, living in the in-between of cultures has produced both challenges and opportunities. Because he looks White he may have an upper hand when it comes to advancing in CHE and navigating Whiteness.

Whiteness and Mission Fit

In this section I decided to treat Whiteness and mission fit together because of the similarities of how they seem to play out in the CCCU. Participants described Whiteness as a way of being, or the dominant culture's preference

---

25. When Ruth spoke of God's diversity and how the missiological table gets bigger, this researcher was recorded stating that he would send her an ofrenda (an offering) for that word. Hallelujah!

26. Josue.

for how things operate, while mission fit relates to the judgement of whether or not someone belongs within the institution due to their capacity to fit in with the norms of the university. Said differently, Whiteness is the normative standard or culture of the university, and mission fit is whether or not a Latinx can assimilate to fit in with a majority culture ethos.

It is important to note that all CCCU schools require faculty and administration to be professing Christians.[27] Most CCCU schools are considered evangelical and have ties to denominations or ethno-religious enclaves that define their missions in doctrinal and political stances, as well as holding particular views of contemporary culture.[28] Latinx leaders not only have to be concerned with discrimination because of their race or ethnicity and the systemic racism that was previously discussed, but also discrimination that is related to their faith traditions and backgrounds.

Ruth, Yanisa, Marisol, and Tomás affirmed that Latinx leaders are often rejected for particular opportunities in CCCU schools because they are not considered to be "mission fit." Mission fit can mean that one does not assimilate to the current culture of the organization or identify fully with the sponsoring denomination, but Ruth stated that the underlining delineation is that "you do not belong here." Describing mission fit further, Moffit states:

> Particularly in religiously-affiliated institutions, denominational preferences could be barriers for those individuals who desire to work at colleges or universities that are affiliated with a church denomination. To ascend to certain levels of leadership, it is not uncommon for some religiously-affiliated institutions to ask candidates vying for executive level positions if they would be willing to switch their church affiliation. In some cases, it is required that all senior level leaders join a church denomination affiliated with their institution. For administrators of color, the barriers could be interpreted as a way for the dominant culture to maintain the balance of power and limit access to underrepresented individuals who are both qualified and competent to successfully lead.[29]

Latinx leaders described that there are many "mission fit" issues for obtaining executive roles. Ruth shared that her experiences have been in stages. Yet, in the current (Trump) political climate, things have definitely changed. In other words, there is a new Pharaoh in town. Ruth explained:

27. Carpenter et al, Christian Higher Education, 271.
28. Carpenter et al, Christian Higher Education, 265.
29. Moffit, "A Narrative Study," 24.

We do the disservice and dehumanization of candidates that meet qualifications, that have the experience, that have the curriculum vita to support what their experience is . . . we take them through the process all the way to the end, and then we say it is not a fit. It's not a missional fit or a community fit. It's not a fit? It's not a fit to what? It's not a fit to the [work] that has been created that only one [specific] group of people fit to. And so, it is a part of the whole reality for me, and I have seen this among my colleagues. I am seeing this right now; I am experiencing this right now as we speak; being a witness of this disservice. Without taking into consideration what that means for the candidates, right? They are left with a lingering message, with a false message that they have worked all the way to the top, but . . . you almost made it. What?! I am sick and tired of the almost made it![30]

Ruth was clear that Latinx are not considered to have "mission fit" because the majority culture who are in power always find something wrong with Latinx candidates. And although a Latina can be fully competent and well-experienced, there is generally something that a committee or group of people find "unfitting" with the Latinx leader.

The very few Latinx that do make it to the executive ranks of Predominately White Institutions (PWIs), are frequently utilized as tokens and not considered people who can bring needed leadership and change. Participants mentioned that tokenism was a reality for them in PWIs. They were either the Latino or Latina that was called to speak on behalf of all Latinx, or they served as the brown reference that was used for marketing or recruitment purposes, or brought forward as the "pepper sprinkled on whiteness" to show that the school had a Latino. All interviewees showcased a disdain for this type of treatment because all considered themselves professionals who had earned their way to leadership positions in Christian higher education (CHE). Marisol compared her CCCU experience to other institutions, and further professed:

I have been in different settings and each setting is different. I have found that in liberal settings you still deal with the racism and so forth, but you are able to have conversations about it much more readily than in evangelical circles. Evangelical circles believe that they are converted so they don't have to deal with the black and white box, or much less the Latino box. But you also have pieces . . . New England is different than the South, more different than the Midwest or even the West. The West is a much different context. It is a much more diverse context. Dealing with the West was a lot easier because diversity was upon them.

Nonetheless, that didn't mean that the way whiteness plays itself out in evangelical schools is by way of theology. They believe that their theology is simply orthodoxy, not recognizing that theology is always worldview. We are all Christians, but we look at the word of God and understand the church through the social location we are coming from. So, theology is our worldview to a certain degree. And when you think that theology is just orthodoxy plain and simple, you don't allow people to have the conversation about race. Instead, theology trumps that conversation and enforces whatever is taking place in the name of orthodoxy and that's how racism continues to perpetuate itself. You will have that in the evangelical schools.[31]

Marisol explained above that evangelical schools think that because they are saved, they are not racist, nor do they discriminate against others. Nonetheless, the participants were in agreement that CCCU schools maintain their predisposition to discriminate because of their theological views, which as we have demonstrated, were established by and through formational Whiteness. Marisol seemed to believe that theology is not neutral but that an individual's sociocultural location, economic status, and traditions play a major role in the way a person sees the world.

Other participants experienced similar attitudes expressed towards them and their particular theological views. If their theological or missiological standpoint was not like a White colleague's, they were dismissed as liberal, or as a person who still had not arrived to their full potential. What occurs when there is no room for conversation or learning? It is clear: anything that challenges the norm of Whiteness is viewed as an attack on the orthodox White gospel. Although the participants did not mention the White Jesus explicitly, this is exactly the construct that the Latinx find themselves struggling against.[32]

31. Marisol.

32. Jun et al, White Jesus, xx. The term White Jesus describes, according to Jun et al, "a socially constructed apparatus . . . that operates stealthily as a veneer for patriarchal White supremist, capitalist, and imperialist sociopolitical, cultural, and economic agendas. White Jesus was constructed by combining empire, colorism, racism, education, and religion—and the byproduct is a distortion that reproduces violence in epistemic and physical ways. We distinguish White Jesus from Jesus of the Gospels, the one whose life, death, and resurrection demands sacrificial love as a response—a love ethic, to be sure—the kind the Prophet Isaiah instructs Hebrew people to follow in chapter 1, verse 17: learn to do good; seek justice, rescue the oppressed, defend the orphan, plead for the widow (Isaiah 1:17 NRSV)."

As mentioned earlier, White Jesus does not give room for other inter-pretations of the gospel since it upholds a Westernized Anglo male-domi-nated view of the world. Yet, the interviewees all stated that their institutions felt that they were either doing all they could to diversify their thinking and operations, or that nothing else was needed because they thought they were well off. When I spoke with Ruth, she really challenged CHE and their diversity claims, although she would agree that some CCCU schools are taking baby steps in the right direction. She shared:

> I think there's some efforts that are being made even with chief diversity officers coming into Christian higher education [and] some trainings that have been in place. I think there's an ef-fort to understand, but there is absolutely nothing going on to the place where the intercultural competency of an institution comes from having enough understanding—the cognitive, that it has an impact on how it behaves [and] on how it changes. This is a time to look at policies . . . processes, to look at what is the framework . . . who is in leadership . . . who and why are those the only people in leadership . . . Who are you building . . . because this is reflective of that. Whoever is within the institu-tion is the kind of people that are investing into the minds of students and then you're producing these kinds of students.
>
> Therefore, what kind of students are you producing be-cause it is a reflection of the kind of institution that you are. And are we really producing globally minded students? How are we producing those globally-minded students? And how can we dare say we're producing globally-minded students and not have a board of trustees that reflects that, not have execu-tive leadership, not have cabinet members that reflect them? Subsequently, for me there's all these checkpoints . . . what are your financial statements saying? We understand this from a missions perspective . . . so we go into churches and we do all this consulting work and we talk about, hey man if this money line item is not reflective of what your mission statement is, than from that perspective there needs to be a change. And I think the same thing applies with Christian higher education. How are you financially investing?[33]

For Ruth, there was much conversation going on but there were not enough strategic efforts that would allow for tangible change for CCCU schools. Participants stated at various times how tiresome committee and task force efforts had become, since there was never a substantial budget to support

33. Ruth.

the work that was needed, let alone emotional support from the highest leadership levels. Participants also stated the need to have diversity present in the board of trustees, executive positions, the president's cabinet, and throughout the staff and faculty.

Participants talked about Latinx having to deal with Whiteness and mission fit fatigue. It is always understood for Latinx that if they do not assimilate, they could lose their job. Latinx always have to prove themselves, because at some level, they are always suspect. Since there are mostly White people in the executive ranks of CCCU schools, comparing the experience of Latinx leaders, Marisol explained that White leaders may not ever have to go through the additional burdens, or be required to behave in the way a Latinx leader would:

> For those who are White . . . they may not ever have to make that decision and as people who are not White going into an institution at whatever level, we need our grounding, we need our community, because racism exhibits itself differently in different people in that institution. There are always the people who are just mean-spirited, they're bullies, they're racist bullies, and they will say things to you and you have to understand where that's coming from in them, and whatever reaction you're having you have to understand where that's coming from in you. And you have to understand that you're going to have good days and bad days in terms of how you are able to navigate those kinds of racist bullies. But your grounding also determines how you navigate, and your community of support also determines that.[34]

She further stated:

> Even further, the problem is that they have taught us to think that [White theology] is the only true parameter for sound doctrine. And people are fearful to leave that because they are no longer in sound doctrine. But they have never realized or asked who has defined it for them, and it has become authoritative voices that have been internalized from generation to generation. And they are embedded . . . and the CCCUs continue to propagate this notion . . . and so if you're going to be a professor or administrator in that setting that's what you are dealing with.[35]

Marisol revealed that at times Latinx leaders question systems, policies, and practices that get showcased as normative, but that may go against who they are. In Marisol's view, White theology is normative in the CCCU and

34. Marisol.
35. Marisol.

anything that does not align with it is considered unfit or not mission fit. Participants stated that mission fit at times is as simple as agreeing (or not) with a certain denomination and the ways in which they operate. And while there are many items that would be acceptable for Latinx to agree with or abide by, at other times there are elements that might go against an individual's ethics or values.

Josue further reflected on his overall experiences along with the experiences of other Latinos in CHE with the following affirmations:

> There is a philosophical support for [Latinos] and their leadership but I don't think that there is a clear understanding of what that means and what kind of transformation has to happen at the institution for that support to be played out fully. I think what you would hear is "we want you here, we want to be more welcoming," but I think it was very difficult to operationalize that desire at a lot of institutions. You know . . . perhaps . . . even systemic cultural bias and other things at work I think it's possible . . . I think it's likely . . . most Latinx leaders with whom I speak would say that it's probably true.
>
> If I went to a campus that had a center that was multicultural or a Hispanic office, you know, those were very rare so you didn't see places that were very dedicated, and when you did, you know, they weren't prominent. They didn't have direct lines to the president . . . they didn't have that operational piece, you know . . . if you want to operationalize this and make it effective and you said, well what's your strategy for recruiting more Hispanic faculty, or how do you support student leadership at your institution for Latina or Latinos? That was not as clear and they were almost surprised to hear that was being asked . . . [he further stated] "we want you to come [and] we want you to bring more Hispanic students to us," but the idea of reframing the entire institution, that was something novel.[36]

Josue's narrative exemplifies what all participants labeled as philosophical support but no real backbone to diversity efforts within their CCCU schools or overall experience. CHE seems to desire people of color in leadership roles and seems to desire more students of color. These Latinx leaders, however, experienced only "surface" support for such diversification, which warrants questions related to the authenticity of the CCCU. It seems to me that Whiteness and the notion of being or not being "mission fit" largely comes down to this question: Will a person of color, and in this specific case Latinx, assimilate and conform to White theology and Westernized

36. Josue.

thinking or not? Because if this person will not conform, they may not be able to make it to the executive level. And if they do make it into the top echelons of leadership, if they challenge White Jesus, they may be out of a job.

The real issue the participants laid out is identified in Josue's final quote above: " 'we want you to come [and] we want you to bring more Hispanic students to us,' but the idea of reframing the entire institution, that was something novel." The idea of having Latinx leadership does not seem to come from genuine interest in who the Latinx are and what they might bring in terms of transformational leadership, but rather whom they may attract to the institution in terms of people of color. Tokenism plays a large part in Latinx landing executive roles but not because they are considered competent and experienced. If Latinx were hired because of a true reception of their competence and experience, perhaps the way the whole institution operates would be open for reframing and transformation.

Unfortunately, Whiteness plays a major role when determining if Latinx will be successful or not in the CCCU. According to the participants, unless Latinx assimilate to the norms of White Jesus, they are basically marginalized and targeted as an outsider. "Mission fit," then, becomes a standard for Latinx and other executives to live up to if they want to be in the "good boys" club. Anything that transgresses the bounds of Whiteness-shaped Christianity is seen or felt as a threat to the normativity of White privilege and dominance.

The next section deals with the Latinas that were interviewed and their experience as women in a male-dominated context. The glass ceiling, as we will see, is present.

The Glass Ceiling

Latina women have several challenges in CHE due to the intersectionality of their identity as people of color, on top of the challenges particular to being Latina, and having to deal with the complexity of the glass ceiling. Yanisa, Marisol, Ruth and even Tomás spoke on the issues women encounter in CHE, from racism to sexism, and to White male normative ideologies. Marisol, Yanisa, and Ruth were the only Latinas in the executive leadership at their universities, which makes it easy to imagine the isolation they felt. When addressing the need for women Latina leaders, Gómez de Torres asserts:

> The need for programs or institutes that can develop and prepare new Latina leaders is evident. However, those programs need to tailor to the different Latina leaders' needs to meet different

needs: emotional intelligence, communication skills, how to network, how to use a coping mechanism, learning and under-standing about leadership attributes and skill, learning about the administrative system, how to implement a transformative learning approach, and finally, how to effectively navigate the two cultures without losing sense of who they are.[37]

The glass ceiling is still very prevalent in CHE.[38] Latinas have to deal with systemic issues in the CCCU as female leaders. Yanisa mentioned it was twice as difficult if you served in the diversity, equity, and inclusion (DEI) field. Dealing with leadership change and systems in CHE as women can be strenuous, agreed Ruth and Yanisa.

Regarding sexism, Yanisa stated, "when I get upset or aggravated in a meeting, it's like . . . you are getting emotional. So, I am not supposed to play out emotions, but when men do so it's considered righteous anger. Women are not supposed to get angry in Christian higher education." All female interviewees explained that sexism and prejudice are definite realities for them in the CCCU. They have to be able to speak multiple languages in their institutions, such as male-dominated ideologies and political specificities of the organization, and they must have the ability to jump in and out of the majority culture. All of this has to be accomplished without revealing much emotion since emotion is categorized as feminine and not leaderlike. Gó-mez de Torres stated that women in higher education will need support to grow in their leadership and must receive encouragement to be themselves without feeling ostracized.[39] But the reality for Latina women is that they navigate multiple intersections of identity such as gender, race and ethnicity, besides the added burdens of organizational policy and CCCU culture. Marisol further declared:

> But then there is a lack of ethics . . . they don't know how to think ethically because the parameters are very thin on the ethical side. As long as you don't smoke, dance and run women, you are good . . . I'm thinking of a young woman who is tremendously talented who lost her job at one of those institutions because she said, "hey, you've been doing this, and if you continue to do this when you have to report this, this and this will happen . . . let's correct this. [This transpired within the financial aid office] I'm bringing this to your attention so that we can correct this, this is what we need to do to correct this." And they said to her, "well,

37. Gómez de Torres, "Latina Leaders," 144.

38. Ruth, Marisol, Yanisa.

39. Gómez de Torres, "Latina Leaders," 144.

is that what you really think, that that's what we have to do?"
And because she thought so . . . they wanted her to cover up for
them . . . but she was not going to cover up for them . . . so she
lost her freaking job![40]

Marisol revealed that this young female leader lost her job because she was
not willing to abide by the (unethical) practices of the university, and also
felt ostracized because she was a woman. All the Latina participants stated
that being a woman actually works against you in the CCCU since it is a
male-dominated system. Tomás mentioned that he was a huge supporter of
women in executive leadership within the CCCU and tried to advocate for
women by all means necessary: "I am a big proponent for women in leadership and I carry that out."

The female participants and Tomás all expressed the difficulty for
women leading in the CCCU, since the normal standard for leadership has
been White and male. The glass ceiling is a concept that seems like an unspoken rule within schools. Although some women are allowed in and may
even be offered a place at the table, there still subsist issues of equity and
inclusion that keep them restricted to certain attainments for leadership.
Many times their leadership is questioned, and they are not seen, or at least
they do not feel equal to men; especially White men.

The next section of this chapter presents the theological and missiological frameworks that guide Latinx in the CCCU. This represents a unique
contribution to higher education and Latinx studies since most experiences
are detailed from public institutions. In this research, leaders' faith and how
it relates to their leadership and service is presented.

THEOLOGICAL AND MISSIOLOGICAL FRAMEWORKS

This section explores what theological or missiological frameworks drive
executive Latinx leaders in CHE. As mentioned previously, many CCCU
schools belong to denominations and have commensurately unique ways
of operating. But Latinas all come from very diverse theological traditions,
so exploring their theological foundations and traditions and how they play
out in CHE is imperative.

My intention was to explore how Latinx leaders think theologically
and act missiologically in Christian higher education (CHE). Since research
is very limited in this area, my hope is that this can serve as a source of

---

40. Marisol. This story actually gets worse, but I have decided not to include
more information from the interview in order to keep this young woman's identity
anonymous.

inspiration for Latinx and other people of color. Thus, a look at Latinx theology and missiology through interviews provides fresh insight for the Latinx reader who may be struggling with their theology in their leadership practice in the CCCU. Additionally, these perspectives may bring revelation and understanding to the majority culture in the CCCU about the Christian Latinx community. A few themes were evident while interviewing participants, including the concepts of justice, dependence on the Holy Spirit, and a faith that is driven through intense prayer.

Justice and Faith

All the Latinx interviewed were from diverse theological traditions. While one may seem to be more conservative in some respects than the others, all had charismatic overtones. Though all expressed their faith from charismatic perspectives, one common theme united them as they talked about expressing their faith, and this was justice. Tomás clarified his theological experience in the following way:

> I will always operate from my own theological context. I am not sure that there's a framework that encompasses all Latinx administrators in this particular case. I think it would be predicated on the individual and their theological upbringing. . .I am a Methodist from a Free Methodist background. That is my theological bent. This is the way that my Christian worldview is shaped, the doctrine associated with Free Methodism and what that means. Therefore, I lean towards the oppressed, the marginalized, and the poor. I am a big proponent for women in leadership and I carry that out. Because I am a Methodist, prevenient grace is often times my approach to leadership, and an opportunity to find grace in the middle of chaos and messiness of life . . . I say there is grace that can overcome it all.[41]

Tomás expressed what all interviewees seemed to hold in common: a faith that was practiced in the public community. This was not a private faith or a mere focus on trying to uphold the correct doctrine; this was an active faith that benefitted those with whom interviewees came into contact. All participants mentioned that their faith drove them to "lean towards the oppressed, the marginalized, and the poor."

Institutions that belong to the CCCU mostly consider themselves "Christ-centered" or identify as institutions that deliver a "Christ-centered

41. Tomás.

education."[42] One of the prerequisites for membership status in the CCCU is the capacity for institutions to incorporate faith in their curriculum. This means the school has to integrate the Bible into all programs of the university. When asked about faith and CHE, Marisol declared:

> Christian higher education began as a way of addressing issues of justice. That's how it began. Giving people access to education. Helping people get jobs. Teaching the children of immigrants. The evangelical church was a part of all of that. *Que se han olvidado es otra cosa*[43] . . . Charles Finney did not give the communion to people who had slaves because he would say that they were in sin. And until they repented, he did not give them the communion. He had revivals all over.
>
> Then people moved to open churches in the South, and when they moved to open churches in the South, they preached to those Southern people out there and they got lynched. They gave their life to believe in a radical gospel. That is the evangelical church and we need to look back to that. *La pobreza de hoy no tiene color.*[44] That's one of the biggest pieces that we are going to have to deal with . . . poverty. And if we don't deal with issues of poverty, and ask ourselves how we serve to create infrastructure that's based on the poor and the infrastructure of solidarity . . . the models that we have are not sustainable.[45]

Marisol conveyed her frustration with CHE and implied that it had lost its original impetus for existence. She was not the only Latinx leader who felt this way. All participants stated that they served in CHE because of the historic mission, but that at times this mission was not experientially clear. In other words, CCCU schools seemed to be misleading constituents, since there were signs that they had drifted from their original mission and vision. Marisol mentioned that former evangelical leaders gave their lives for the radical gospel. I was left wondering: Does this occur today? Or do we simply curate a business that is dressed as Christian in order to sell a product that does not fully deliver?

During my interview with Marisol, she explained that Latinx leaders need to have an inner authority and understand that administrators cannot fight every battle. Said differently, choosing wisely what battles to get involved in is essential:

42. Litfin, Conceiving the Christian College, 35–36; Carpenter et al, Christian Higher Education, 268.

43. "That they have forgotten is another subject."

44. "Today's poverty does not have a color."

45. Marisol.

Administration has to be for people who know how to be decisive, people who know how to have a non-anxious presence and who have an inner authority. You have to have an inner authority because you can't have integrity unless you have an inner authority. Hence, your points of decision are going to depend on ways you develop your sense of self, and your sense of self gives you a sense of inner authority, and that's going to be based on your sense of integrity and accountability.

In both cases, you have to establish a grounding and a support community for yourself. In any case, whether you are faculty or whether you are administration, if you are a person who is not a part of the dominant culture of that institution, you must know what your values are, because they are going to determine on what hill you are willing to die . . . you can't fight all the battles but you have to determine on what hill you're going to be willing to die . . . when you do it, you know [not] because you're . . . heroic, but because given your integrity and your values, this is the hill that you're willing to die [on].[46]

Most participants mentioned that Latinx leaders cannot fight every battle. Choosing battles wisely also meant not being tagged as the angry person of color on campus who is always mad or bitter. Choosing which battles they would fight—and which battles they would release—seemed to be determined by what impacted those who had no voice or those who were the most vulnerable within their sphere of influence and responsibility. In other words, they would fight for what they thought aligned with God's justice. Justice driven by their faith was vital.

Justice work is not always easy or the most popular thing to do. According to Yanisa, Latinx leaders have to keep the bigger picture in perspective. For example, Yanisa reflected on her theological and missional practice and stated:

My theological and missional thing hasn't changed but I think my pragmatic piece has reminded me of Christ who says "render unto Caesar what's Caesar's, and to the Lord what's his." And so I have to let go of my demand for justice in a human way, and trust the Lord will do his justice in another way. That's one example. The other example is that even though I'm getting pushed in a very White privileged way for diversity to get done, someone reminded me of the story of Jairus and the woman with the issue of blood . . . remember that story? Jairus is saying come to my house . . . who's a very high-ranking person

46. Marisol.

. . . and he says, come to my house, my daughter is sick unto death . . . so in the middle of that he's asking Jesus to come to him. Jesus stops and asks, "who touched me, who touched me?" Because the woman who had been an outcast, who not only was a woman, she was also a bleeding woman, which made her [a] completely unclean person . . . Jesus interrupts the conversation with the higher-up . . . the privileged person . . . He interrupts that to pay attention to the least.

So, it feels like in this moment we are in that moment that says: we are interrupting the privileged to pay attention to those that are weakest . . . who had courage to touch him, who had faith to touch him . . . who still believed that he could heal her but she knew she couldn't do it in the same way this high privileged man could. But [Jesus] cares enough about her that he turns to her and interrupts that, stops it, and says woman you are healed . . . and then he goes back to Jairus, because you don't want to totally blow off the White privileged person, but you want to teach them something.

So part of me responding to the president and responding to these demands to do this and to do that and do it now . . . part of me has to say to him, wait, I have to deal with the crying of my pain-filled colleagues of color, and I'm doing that now so you need to wait, which is what I did, I said to him wait. So I attended to that and we did some work etc. Now I can turn back to him and say ok . . . yes, we will do that and here's the way it's going to get done. But it doesn't negate that he also watched me turn and care for the least. Somehow that story is part of my faith narrative . . . in my flesh I want to say heck with the White privileged person . . . but that's not right. We need them to change too . . . in that story I was reminded that God cares for both of these people, the woman and man, but he still cares for him. [So] it doesn't mean that we get to ignore them as well.[47]

Yanisa mentioned in this quote that she at times did not want to help the privileged person, but because Jesus did, she said we should also. She stated that following the Lord's example was a good model to use. Jesus helped the hurting woman and helped the privileged man. In other words, in imitating Jesus, people of color should help both the needy and vulnerable *and* those that are in power. The participants all seemed to be doing this since they were all serving from a marginalized place, but also were attentive to those who were considered the least among them.

47. Yanisa.

The prophetic work of justice through praxis and faith takes intentionality, according to the interviewees. People who need justice and mercy are all around, but leaders must position themselves to serve. Josue further declared:

> I think the call for true justice . . . we needed and need to be at the vanguard of those discussions instead of being at the trailer . . . we need to be at the forefront of that. The heart of Jesus was to go to the Samaritan woman and that's not where we have been, we just haven't . . . and part of it for me is intentionality . . . what would it mean if we said as CCCU schools and affiliates, if we said that we're going to institute a requirement . . . something around multiculturalism, or you name the term—diversity, the idea of the fullness of the Kingdom . . . what would that be? If the police force said they're never going to use the chokehold, which is a very small starting point, what would that small starting point be with the CCCU? That's what I would say, that the time is not to have another conference, let's not have the task force, let's just say we're going to do this thing, we're going to do this one thing . . . take an action to change what we have done in the past.
>
> I think God uses these moments where the pressure builds and builds and it builds then the pressure explodes . . . when you got thousands of people in the streets in Paris because of something that happened in Minnesota, to me God's in that, God's working something deep there even with COVID-19 they didn't care . . . they're going to get out there and say, this is too important to just sit in my room.[48]

At the time of this writing, the general society is facing several crises—the COVID19 pandemic and its multiple variants, racial unrest in U.S. cities due to police brutality, economic crisis, and drastic climate change. Josue declared that the CCCU should seize the moment swiftly by addressing justice issues, discontinuing its silence. He pointed out that the police force has made a small adjustment to their practices in order to address systemic racism: namely, eliminating the chokehold. Josue then further stated: "If the police force said they're never going to use the chokehold, which is a very small starting point, what would that small starting point be with the CCCU?" He then went on to say that we did not need any more committees or task forces, alluding to the amount of time it takes and the distraction that it actually is to productive change and transformation.

The participants spoke in one voice about racial justice moving at the speed of a caterpillar—very slowly. No one expressed happiness or

48. Josue.

contentment with the CCCU's attempt to address racial disparities, diversity issues at large, or justice work overall. Everyone expressed disappointment because there was a belief that the CCCU could in fact do better. Ruth posed the question: if we continue to move at the pace that we are moving, will we ever get anywhere in terms of diversity, equity, and inclusion? Participants were also straightforward about the fact that their ministry in the CCCU did not necessarily depend on others, because they were working towards a higher calling. Their calling was to do right before God and to do the work of justice.

Tomás thought that CHE in the twenty-first century could and should do better in terms of justice and felt that the CCCU was lagging behind secular institutions in demonstrating empathy and compassion. Regarding current events, Tomás further stated:

> Christian higher education needs to be sending the letter that the commissioner from the NFL sent, Roger Goodell, and admitted wrong publicly in terms of how they handled the Kaepernick situation. I believe Christian higher education needs to be doing the same. There's a ton of letters that still need to be written that they have not written. There's a ton of apologies publicly that need to take place that have not taken place. There's a ton of confession—so think about it theologically—to what degree [is] Christian higher education truly confessing their sins of perpetuation of systemic racism and potential oppression to people of color on their campuses? But because they want to cover the sun with one finger they don't do it.
>
> To what degree are Christian higher education institutions truly embracing matters of justice, not just diversity and inclusion because it's the popular thing to do, but really trying to change the narrative by creating systemic changes within their institutions? Not many! Not many! . . . We presented at the diversity conference at the CCCU and I basically shouted out from mountain tops . . . the day in which presidents get fired for not doing this work is the day in which change will take place . . . This needs to be a fireable cause, a just cause to fire a president at this stage particularly in Christian higher education. There should be no more passivity around it and a clear message needs to be delineated [but] it has not been done. Christian higher education continues to be passive . . . Christian higher education continues to be second, third, fourth in response . . . Christian higher education is not leading in the matter; we are actually responding. And we could lead, we could get out there . . .[49]

49. Tomás.

Tomás was very clear that CHE was not leading in matters of justice but was in fact lagging behind secular institutions like the NFL. Other participants also mentioned the NBA and even public higher education. This seemed somewhat satirical since the CCCU is Christian and Christians should uphold biblical justice. But the issue remains that the board and administrative leadership of universities do not yet see diversity issues as substantive biblical matters. This was a major frustration for the participants. The conflict within the participants was palpable. On the one hand, the CCCU is Christian, and Christians should care deeply about matters of justice, but on the other hand the participants did not experience this as a priority for CCCU leadership overall. These Latinx leaders hold a collective amount of 128 years of experience. This experience has led to disappointment regarding the ways in which the CCCU treats (or ignores) issues of diversity, equity, and justice.

Tomás also mentioned that this work would be taken earnestly the day executives (like presidents) in the CCCU got fired for not addressing issues of justice and diversity. This is a strong statement since it also touches on other challenges pointed out by other participants, including the lack of adequate accountability for leadership, the lack of substantial budgets for diversity work, and the lack of adequate pipelines for people of color for executive leadership positions. At first glance these seem to be different matters, but according to the participants these issues all stem from the same issue—the lack of interest in and commitment to promoting equity.

Ruth seemed to think that persons who participate in majority culture are not the only ones culpable for the current reality. When speaking about current events, faith, and how to respond as Christians, Ruth mentioned that Latinos also need to do better:

> As Latinos we have to use our voting privileges wisely, and then at the same time as I say that, it has just overwhelmed me the number of Latinos who are in favor of the current [Trump] administration and are not able to see the inequities. I mean it leaves me in a real awe . . . I also think that us as Latinos have to think broader, we have to think . . . I mean we're [a] collective community and caring for our brothers and sisters has to be important.
>
> And every time I hear about a Hispanic American protesting immigration and talking about how what is happening in the jails where they are being detained, "like you broke the law you pay for it," there's something wrong with this picture, you are completely disconnected from the realization. And you can't ignore [that] mass incarceration is the new Jim Crow . . .

I mean, how can we not think that we won't be accountable to God for that?[50]

For Ruth, there are some Latinos who have bought into the notion of Whiteness. And this is understandable in one way, since assimilating does lead to success in the U.S. (in many cases, above less assimilated brothers and sisters). But Ruth seemed to think that this was selling out of *la Raza*,[51] or your own community. It is one thing for White people to not care about issues of justice, but for Ruth, it seemed unheard of for a person of color or Latinx to be conducting themselves in this manner. She believed that persons in these communities should know better, and because Latinx understood the struggles, Latinx could and should sympathize more fully. It is important to note that none of the interviewees condoned illegal behavior or riots, or any other criminal acts. However, the participants seemed to think that pursuing equity was necessary, calling out the wrong was vital, and calling out injustices was essential.

There are many things that cause division in the body of Christ and in CHE. Serving the poor, as described by Marisol, immigration reform, as mentioned by Ruth, justice for Black and Brown people as presented by Tomás, or equality for women, as emphasized by Yanisa and others, all are factors. People like to be around people who are familiar.[52] Although research has shown that diverse groups produce a greater level of innovation,[53] the CHE enterprise has been slow in its development towards a more inclusive environment.

Change and innovation hold promise for CHE, and the CCCU specifically. Jesus taught, *"no one pours new wine into old wineskins. Otherwise, the wine will burst the skins, and both the wine and the wineskins will be ruined. No, they pour new wine into new wineskins"* (Mark 2:22, NIV). It is going to require a new wine (a new way of thinking) and new wineskins (new systems, structures, and policies) for CHE to lead in diversity efforts and in the creation of more equitable campuses. Latinx leaders show promise through their faith-driven justice work and can become a model for the CCCU to follow. An example of this would be Ruth and her consultancy firm. Through her experiences, education and leadership, she has been able to provide leadership development and diversity and inclusion services to majority-culture-led institutions. She and her team have been able to come

50. Ruth.

51. "The Race" or "your people."

52. Cleveland, Disunity in Christ, 29.

53. Cleveland, Disunity in Christ, 39; Livermore, Driven by Difference, 2; Willams, Strategic Diversity Leadership, 31; Wildavsky et al, Reinventing Higher Education, 11–13.

alongside schools, denominations, and other diverse organizations, equipping them with the tools to become culturally responsive, justice-driven, and equity-minded.

The next section of this chapter presents some particulars of the faith of these Latinx leaders, in terms of prayer and their reliance on the Holy Spirit as themes that stood out when they were interviewed.

Prayer and Dependence on the Holy Spirit

This section of the chapter presents perspectives on Latinx spirituality. Although there exists no cookie-cutter approach to theology from Latinx, there is some common ground on how church is experienced. Tomás asserted that there are charismatic influences in the Latinx Methodist church, while in other Methodist circles it may not be so. Further testifying that the Latinx church teaches congregants about hard work, dedication, and perseverance, Tomás explained that his leadership and spiritual formation were inspired by this type of church.

Josue, Ruth, and Marisol all believed that the struggles in CHE enabled Latinx leaders to know God deeper. Ruth testified that through trials and tribulations, we learn who we are as a people. Our ancestors had to go through many struggles for Latinx leaders to be who they are, and to go where they are going. This is what shapes us spiritually. "We needed God to make [some] miracles. We have come from places where God has shown up where there wasn't any milk. And someone showed up with milk. How can we forget that? That shaped our spiritual formation."[54] Ruth shared that Latinas grew up fasting and praying because they had no other choice. "We cannot lose this in the current mix of division and spirituality of the United States."[55] When Tomás was asked about his spiritual formation, he professed:

> When I think of spiritual formation, I think to the degree to how I can experience God through discipleship and prayer, scripture reading and streams of freshness, holiness, and justice. That is the way that I see the world and how I engage it. I engaged the world through seeking first the kingdom of God and all of its justice, then everything is added to you and your family, and everyone around you. That's how I see my spiritual formation. Lastly, dedication to prayer because there is so many confusing faiths that come at you as a Latino. This may not be anyone else's experience, but I am just giving you mine . . . You are bound to

54. Ruth.
55. Ruth.

walk on your knees all the time until you are formed spiritually through the seeking of who you are in the context of the environment, because the environment forces you to be prayerful.[56]

Tomás was clear that the CCCU was an environment in which Latinx needed to consistently maintain a prayer life. As he stated, "You are bound to walk on your knees all the time until you are formed spiritually through the seeking of who you are in the context of the environment, because the environment forces you to be prayerful." The difficulties that Latinx leaders encounter in Christian higher education (CHE) are abundant; therefore, living a life of prayer and fasting was important for Latinx leaders. The participants demonstrated that they did not operate on their own or try to lead on their experience or intellect alone, but depended totally on the Holy Spirit.

When Ruth was asked about what was needed by Latinx in terms of faith, in order to contribute to a more inclusive environment in the CCCU, she declared a "theology of other" was essential. Ruth stated that God created diversity, and we should celebrate it. Even within the Latinx community there is division, according to Ruth. She affirmed, "we need to recognize that the system is flawed, but we need to learn how to respect and honor each other." Christena Cleveland underscores, "diverse groups that fully live out the biblical mandate to unite under one household . . . will reap the benefits of increased learning, increased creativity and more effective problem solving."[57] There are echoes of this in Ruth's declaration: "Everything is different when you see it from the lenses of God:" Ruth further explained:

> You've got Genesis and you've got Revelation, and in both the beginning and the end there is this message that is weaved from the beginning all the way to the end about God's diversity, that it's about that creativity, that it's about God's abundance of offering unto us this beautiful buffet and opportunities and different ways of looking at life. And that takes itself all the way to the last book of the Bible at this great vision of heaven being filled with all kinds of people from all kinds of places. And for me that is the most obvious framework weaved into all of that, is this reality that somewhere along the line right there there's been this message, and perhaps a misinterpretation of a message that has created this fact that there's an us and them.
>
> But then you land on the book of Acts, which for me is transformational. And you begin to see the things that are happening in Acts, there's so many revolutionary things happening in Acts,

56. Tomás.

57. Cleveland, *Disunity in Christ*, 40.

from Jesus ascending and giving power to go everywhere—Jerusalem, Judea, Samaria, and to the ends of the earth . . . from the outpour of the Holy Spirit, from the spreading of the people, from Saul and this blindness that's being unveiled from him . . . Peter having this vision and being in a trance and watching this white sheet come down from heaven and challenging his cultural and religious belief; and the voice telling him to get up, kill and to eat and for him being rebellious, saying "no way am I going to do any other things, my lips are pure, they're clean, I have protected myself from being tainted and of being with the gentiles," right. . .and of hanging out and eating with those people and God in this voice is telling him "no that is not the image that I have of the gentiles," and then God breaking that in him and him being able to break bread with the gentiles.

And then a few chapters later Paul had to call him on it, hello! You just finished being a revolutionary figure in the move of reconciling gentiles and Jews and here you go again, now you're stuck in and trapped in this place again? And so just recognizing that it's an up and down movement . . . apart from the Holy Spirit, every single example that you will find in the Old and New Testament happens only one way . . . in a deep connection with God. Therefore . . . everything is different when you're seeing it through the lens of God . . . everything![58]

Ruth had a deep sense that the Holy Spirit was always moving and working. She revealed that "everything is different" when the Holy Spirit is involved. This was a profound statement since she was alluding to diversity work in the CCCU, and how faith should lead that work. Participants were clear that their dependence was on what the Holy Spirit said, and how the Holy Spirit would expect them to act. Ruth's exegesis of scripture above explains how she saw the work of God in and through the church, and how she expected CHE to operate from this type of praxis.

Ruth also challenged this "us and them" mentality or interpretation of the scriptures. By her explanation of Acts 2 and all that the Holy Spirit had accomplished throughout the church and apostles, she was in essence saying that this is how we should be functioning today—in unity. The work and ministry of the Holy Spirit unites and binds us together, according to Ruth, and through Jesus Christ we are reconciled to one another and God. This would be the work of the Holy Spirit in diversity work—through constant communication and prayers, and dependence on what the Spirit can and will do.

58. Ruth.

When Josue was asked about his theology or missiology throughout his service in the CCCU, he testified:

> When I came to Christian higher education, I realized that there was a greater responsibility for me to ground myself even further in the word. It's funny because it shouldn't have mattered since it is all a mission field . . . I spent more time in prayer and reading God's word; more time in understanding different theological perspectives. Again, working in the secular context, I did not need to understand the nuances between Wesley versus Brethren, versus . . . you name it . . . it was not important. But now it seems far more important. Now students can say to me, I'm Southern Baptist or I'm whatever have you . . . or ask what elements in my theology trouble you or excite you? And I did not think it was appropriate for an executive leader to say, I don't know much about that.
>
> It's funny, people said to me if you ever work in a Christian context, you will likely meet the most dedicated and Christian people you've ever known. And you will likely be hurt more deeply in this context than any other context you have worked in your life. And the people who said that to me were right.[59]

Josue's description of seeking God intensely while serving in the CCCU was reflected in all the participants' testimonies. There was a shared sense that it is necessary to have a deep intimacy with the Holy Spirit in order to lead and serve well. And although these contexts are explicitly Christian, the conflict and resistance a Latinx will face provide further necessity for the need to "walk on their knees" as Tomás stated.

Finally, Josue mentioned that before he transitioned to CHE from public higher education, he was told that he would meet some great people and have wonderful colleagues. He confirmed this to be true. He also mentioned that he was told, "And you will likely be hurt more deeply in this context than any other context you have worked in your life." He also affirmed these statements. Unfortunately, all the participants had similar accounts of their experiences within CHE, and they all seemed to be emerging from a core of injustice. In other words, their difficult times were not necessarily from hard work due to the rigor of working in CHE, but from the added pressures of struggling with a racially broken system. This is why interviewees had such a strong impetus to pray and to depend on the Holy Spirit.

The next section of this chapter focuses on the questions asked to the Latinx leaders pertaining to their leadership practices in CHE.

59. Josue.

LEADERSHIP NEEDED BY EXECUTIVE
LATINX LEADERS

This book has been based on the following primary questions to Latinx leaders:

1. What are the experiences of Latinx administrators in the CCCU?

2. What theology and missiology drives Latinx leaders in the CCCU?

3. What leadership is needed by Latinx leaders to flourish in the CCCU?

4. What am I not asking that I need to know; or what else do you want to share with me overall?

5. How do current events of systemic racism affect Christian higher education (CHE)?

We turn now to the leadership practices of Latinx leaders in CHE.

I myself have had varied leadership and follower experiences in the CCCU, and it has been my task to understand what type of leadership is best suited to the CHE context. Since there are very few executive Latinx leaders in the CCCU, it is important to collect their stories and experiences, in order to illuminate contextual challenges and truths for up-and-coming Latinx leaders who could learn from and emulate what these established leaders have lived. This section, therefore, presents starting points for defining executive Latinx leadership in CHE.

Latinx Leadership

The executive Latinx leaders interviewed explained that leadership is complicated in the CCCU, mainly because of the structures in higher education, their bicultural nature and self-identity, internal and external confusion, and lack of mentors.[60] The difficulty intensifies when Latinx leaders become fatigued from having to navigate a PWI mostly alone in the executive ranks. All Latinx leaders were asked about their leadership, and were asked particularly to identify what intercultural, multicultural, or contextual leadership was needed to navigate this complexity. Several themes emerged when interviewing the Latinx leaders concerning their leadership, primarily: (1) collaborative and community-driven leadership, (2) lifelong learning, and (3) "chameleon," contextual and code-switching leadership.

---

60. Marisol, Ruth, Yanisa, Tomás, Josue.

Collaborative and Community-Driven Leadership

The participants all lead from a frame of valuing service, relationship-building, and collaboration. Marisol explained that it was the relational pieces that helped her in her leadership. In doing the work of higher education, "the work," according to Marisol, needs to be student-centered. She asserted that it was not only good to serve students, but that also leaders need to know their students personally. According to A. Núñez et al, institutions need to invest in understanding Latinx students and their unique contextual needs to better serve them. This includes the "cultural, social, economic, and political issues that affect Latino students." They further explain, "it involves building trust with the student and valuing the student's cultural background and assets."[61]

Marisol declared that building relationships with others was most important to her theologically. "This is how you find what people's needs are." Josue stated that God gave him a word of knowledge that Hispanic students chose his classes when he was a professor simply because of his name. In other words, they knew that he would be able to relate to them. This supports Marisol and Josue's observation that Latinx students gravitate toward schools where they see themselves represented in the leadership of the school.

The relational piece is transformational and important, according to Marisol. She declared that we grow spiritually through relationships. This kind of relational cultivation includes deep reflection and careful listening to others. "If you want to have power but don't like people, don't get into this," declared Marisol. Things get done with people for people. In other words, effective leadership is based on relationship-building. It calls you to get out of your comfort zone and focus on service. In the incarnational process of relationships, even with students who are not Christian, one's life and theology will forever be changed, according to Marisol. Said differently, building relationships and being present within the community is the only way for Latinx to lead and serve.

Ruth declared that Latinx will need to seek their own leadership theories and models, while being comfortable in their own skin. She further asserted that being authentic was essential, and the ability to lead oneself first, before leading others, was an imperative. Having a servant heart and being relentless is Josue's personal leadership preference. The participants explained that getting to know people was important in leading well since this was a people-centered endeavor.

---

61. Núñez et al, Hispanic-Serving Institutions, 37.

Long term investments will have to be made for the community. According to Josue, Latinas are the only group that have not made much progress in higher education leadership circles in the last twenty years. He also stated there may be an issue with accountability or budget constraints at the executive levels. When asked how he led, and how he might recommend that other Latinx lead, he asserted:

> Well, I do believe that having a servant's heart as a leader is the most critical aspect. I mean, if you really know that you're here to serve the Lord first, then you will not compromise. I would suggest that that is the most critical aspect of all, to come in humility and just know that you're there to serve others. Therefore, it's serving God first, serving the mission of the institution, serving the students, and then serving everyone around you. So, I'd say that's the primary factor, but I also believe that if you're relentless about quality you will not allow the truth to be compromised. I think those are two other critical aspects.[62]

Josue was adamant that for Latinx leaders in CHE, refusing to compromise values and focusing on service were crucial. He felt that Latinx leaders needed to have their connection with God intact in order to have their connection with others flourish. He mentioned that executive leaders are there to serve others, plain and simple. There is no other reason for being in leadership but to be a servant and to render one's heart towards the community you are serving. All the interviewees agreed with Josue that Latinx leaders were first servants and that they needed to be with the people, since one was there for that very reason in the first place. But then they also shared that they accomplished this with teams, with other people who served alongside them. No one envisioned themselves leading in isolation.

Another important point Josue made was the necessity of Latinx leaders believing wholeheartedly in the mission and vision of their institutions. The sentiment was that if you do not agree or believe in the organization's mission, it can ultimately affect your service and leadership. All the participants spoke highly of the mission of CHE and believed that this was a specific calling. Marisol further explained how the mission and community worked together in order to lead well:

> And the focus that we make for that mission helps us to work together but the other thing that helps us to work together is that we create spaces to come together to talk about that work together. And where people can bring experiences that they had and where we really listen. And let me tell you, we really listen

62. Josue.

porque este es un trabajo que es[63] heavy-duty, this is heavy lift-
ing. There are no assumptions that we can make in this work . . .
everybody is like . . . anything and everything we can come up
with together, let's do it, because we all need to hear all the best
ideas, because this is hard work.[64]

Marisol asserted that working with colleagues together was the best way to
get things done. Everyone brought ideas and creativity, and Latinx leaders
needed to leverage this innovation. This community-driven leadership at
times can be difficult, especially in the culture of the CCCU. But the Latinx
leaders all seemed to work through this challenge using collaboration as a
blueprint to complete the mission.

Since Tomás was no longer in CHE by 2020, I asked him what was
different about leading in his current place of service. He responded:

It still gives me the opportunity to be in leadership [but] very
different. My senior leadership team . . . you know . . . there is
no White person in it. It's all Latino individuals . . . from different countries [like] Mexico, Dominican Republic, Puerto
Rico, Venezuela . . . Very different leadership role, very different
approach, a very different entity. But very similar needs, very
similar spaces, very similar opportunities, but with none of the
battles of engaging respect, or engaging credibility, [or] engaging any of that kind of stuff.[65]

Tomás stated that in this alternate setting, his credibility was assumed, and
he did not need to prove himself. The main difference between CHE and his
current place of service was that the people he worked with and reported
to him were not White. In this interview with Tomás (2020) I remembered
that in the previous interview with him (2018) he asserted that Latinx leaders always had to prove themselves in CHE. Consequently, I was compelled
to ask him if he felt the same way now in the organization where he was the
CEO, and he responded:

"Oh no, no, no . . . I come with all the credibility in the world. It's actually different in that space because what I do is actually really lean on the
team. The team now responds better because I don't have to necessarily prove
myself to them . . . I've already come with the credibility necessary . . . and so
that proving myself to them is actually an exercise that we don't waste time
with . . . it's more [like], let me empower you to actually do the work that we

63. "Because this is a heavy-duty job."

64. Marisol.

65. Tomás.

believe we can do together and so leadership manifests itself very different right now."[66] Tomás mentioned that he did not need to prove himself as he did when he was in CHE. It appears that he did not need to because all the people he was working with were from diverse backgrounds, and the context was not a White space. In other words, in his new context, he discovered that there was room for everyone to bring themselves and work together in a professional manner, and he is now able to lead by empowering his colleagues to do their work. Tomás doesn't have to fight with an all-White male board of trustees anymore, or worry about being "too Latino," since most people on his team are Latinx and people of color. Tomás explained that he was given his due place as the executive leader. This was quite a contrast to his experience serving at the CCCU, where he always felt that he had to prove himself to people who never had his best interests in mind.

The next section of this chapter deals with the leadership of Latinx and their capacity to remain teachable as lifelong learners.

Lifelong Learners

This section expresses the participants' approach to leadership in the form of learning. Marisol and Yanisa in particular confirmed the importance of relationships through service and leadership. Latinx leaders came across as very relational and authentic in their leadership. And in these connections, they indicated that it was important to learn from others in order to kindle good ties, building social capital and thus furthering the ability to leverage each other's influence.

According to Marisol, leadership is very challenging, and people have to learn and grow continuously. She further stated that becoming a multicultural leader is not a strategy but the journey of a lifetime. Listening is one of the most valuable assets for leaders today in diversity work. But who is listening and who is serving the least of these? This was a concern for all participants.

Experience and training prepare Latinas to assume leadership roles in CHE. Cooper, Cuyjet and Howard-Hamilton in *Multiculturalism on Campus*, stress "administrators and faculty should routinely evaluate their own level of multicultural competence, including attending diversity seminars and workshops annually."[67] According to Tomás, in order for Latinx leaders to be taken seriously in the CCCU, they will need to prepare themselves academically and professionally. Anthony Cruz, in *Latinx/A/OS in Higher*

---

66. Tomás.

67. Cooper et al, Multiculturalism on Campus, 401.

Education, affirmed that Latinas need to obtain doctorates. In the past, in some settings, one could have gotten away without a doctoral degree, but whether a PhD or EdD, or other terminal degree, Latinas will need a doctorate for a senior leadership position in higher education.[68]

In terms of further investment on behalf of Latinx leaders in CHE, Josue stated:

> I think it is a leadership that understands the complexity of the Kingdom of God. When you talk about the fullness of the Kingdom of God, I think that's what any Latinx leader would generally want to see come. If we want the fullness of the Kingdom of God to be expressed then I think that's the kind of leadership that's needed. It does take the kind of leadership that is willing to engage in a long slow process that have extraordinary rewards but it does take a lot of upfront investment.[69]

Josue clarified that Latinx leaders need to be willing to submit to a process. This requires lifelong learning and commitment to the mission and the kingdom of God. It is an investment that Latinx leaders will need to make in order to see the fruits of their labor. In contrast, Josue stated that many times colleges and universities miss the opportunity to have great Latinx leaders on their team because of what they value, and he spoke in terms of treasure, time and talent. He affirmed:

> We have to reframe our expectation as presidents and board members to say, you know, we checked off this box you know . . . the idea of your time, treasure and talent. So we miss the way we represent that you know . . . we misrepresent that. How much of the T of treasure has to just be about dollars . . . we have a treasure, and we know that comes from the Lord and part of it is a diverse voice and we have to put a new emphasis on that as part of treasure. So anyhow, I think that's part of what has changed the discussion.
>
> Again, from my perspective it goes back to what you will find as treasure and what you really believe is in your heart and so your treasure and your heart align. And so, if you see treasure as just capital . . . I think there's social capital, there's a wisdom capital, even this idea of the fullness of the Kingdom of God capital . . . so the idea in that fullness a treasure will come in terms of those dollars, they will come . . . and I think you unlock the treasury truly when you fully reflect the Kingdom of God,

---

68. Batista et al, *Latinx/a/os in Higher Education*, 209.
69. Josue.

and I think when you fall short of that, you may not have the blessing that can come otherwise . . . so from my belief provision follows vision.[70]

According to Josue, Latinx leaders come with other valuable contributions besides just adding to the bottom line. Latinx come with cultural capital, which helps institutions have a diversity of voices and perspectives. They come with social capital and a consciousness that can enable the CCCU to be "woke"[71] to the issues of the day. Latinx leaders bring what other leaders may bring in terms of competence, experience, and a hard work ethic, but Josue makes the point that they also bring unmeasurable assets such as cultural literacy, adaptability, and kingdom wisdom.

In all their learning, Latinx leaders will need to be aware of how they are doing and when to take their breaks. Serving in CHE is not easy, therefore being self-aware is crucial. Yanisa further stated about knowing yourself:

> I see that I'm human like everybody else and I need to pace my-self . . . So I think Latino leaders need to do this by pacing themselves because [racism] is a problem that's been going on since the creation of man, right . . . always the sin of racism, the sin of separation, the sin of others versus us. And so, if we don't pace ourselves and keep ourselves healthy and whole spiritually and physically, we're going to die and will end up in a place where we hate people, and I don't want to hate people . . . so when I'm on that edge all the time, it may be time to get some self-care.[72]

Participants stated that Latinx leaders should be lifelong learners who are developing themselves continuously, listening to others, and taking care of themselves by pacing themselves in CHE. This is all a part of a healthy leadership culture. These interviewees believed that asking many questions and continuously inquiring about others would allow a leader to best learn their context. In other words, leaders learn not by assuming competence, but by persistently seeking to discover insight related to strategic questions.

The next section of this chapter presents the last component of Latinx leadership: chameleon, contextual, and code-switching leadership.

---

70. Josue.

71. "Woke" is a term that Marisol and others used several times to refer to being awakened or enlightened. You are awake or "woke" to the issues and struggles of people of color.

72. Yanisa.

Chameleon and Code-Switching Leadership

This part of the chapter describes what the participants stated as crucial skill-sets for effective leadership within Christian higher education (CHE). Several themes emerged from the data set in terms of their leadership, including chameleon leadership, contextual leadership, and utilizing code-switching.

Latinx leaders take culturally relevant approaches in their leadership and service.[73] These leaders understand that context matters, and that strategies need to be sensitive not only to Latinx students, but also to all other students. Most importantly, Latinx leaders seem to have tremendous skill at adapting to their environments and communicating in-and-across cultures effectively.[74] "Intercultural communication is defined as the symbolic exchange process whereby individuals from two (or more) different cultural communities attempt to negotiate shared meanings in an interactive situation within an embedded societal system."[75] This clearly describes the Latinx leaders that were interviewed, since they all identified that an essential aspect of their leadership was communicating at the intersections of culture and language.

All colleges and universities are communities that should be concerned about students and their success. Núñez et al state: "role models within the Latino community, such as Latino faculty, administrators, or other professionals, can bring an intuitive understanding of how to respond to Latino students' needs, in turn positively influencing these students' college access, persistence, and graduation."[76] Said differently, institutional leadership helps shape the environments in which persons serve, and Latinx leadership positively impacts institutional effectiveness.[77]

When Tomás was asked about his leadership practices, he stated:

> One of the defining labels I have for myself, and perhaps we can do this better than other cultures . . . The word is chameleon. My ability to walk into a setting and not lose who I am. Not lose any of me. From my identity to manifestation of behavior being shifted and adjusted. Not to sell out or to change who you are, but to really manifest a sense of efficacy, efficiency, and competence that gives you the opportunity to actually move forward.

73. Núñez et al, Hispanic-Serving Institutions, 149.

74. Núñez et al, Hispanic-Serving Institutions, 150.

75. Ting-Toomey and Chung, Understanding Intercultural Communication, 24.

76. Núñez et al, Hispanic-Serving Institutions, 63.

77. Núñez et al, Hispanic-Serving Institutions, 136, as cited in Arellano and Padilla, "Academic Invulnerability," and Reyes and Ríos, "Dialoguing."

So how can I get a team of people who have never had a person of color, specifically a Latino, to supervise them, to be influenced, led and motivated and bring vision and all these things . . . ? I have to be able to connect to language, context, and understand my audience . . . I have to understand the language that they speak. So, all of those things are a part of that. Therefore, for me, the word that comes to mind in terms of cross-cultural, intercultural training for Latinos in particular, is your capacity to become a chameleon. You don't lose who you are, you are everything of who you are, and that shows in many ways. Then you are able to make the adjustments necessary in order to influence.[78]

The explanation that Tomás provided for chameleon leadership was a common theme among the Latinx leaders. Though this term was not used exclusively, they all spoke of a similar concept, using phrases like "code-switching" and describing the ability to interact in between cultures. "Leading cross-culturally, then, is inspiring people who come from two or more cultural traditions to participate with you (the leader or leadership team) in building a community of trust and then to follow you and be empowered by you to achieve a compelling vision of faith."[79] In other words, chameleon leadership denotes the ability to communicate bilingually when it comes to the common language people understand, biculturally in terms of the diversity of people that you are serving, and moving the whole team, unit, or division along with you in order to fulfill your mission. This is a skillset often lacking in the quest for diversity in PWIs.

Tomás gives great detail on what it took for him to have a certain level of effectiveness, especially since most of the people that he was leading never had a senior Latinx leader. Hence, Latinx leaders have to be aware of the context and of themselves and their ability to adapt fully, without losing who they are. Participants explained that they had to learn to adapt to the CCCU, but that that process of learning and adaptation has not been reciprocal.

Latinx leaders have lived in the "in-between" much of their lives, from their communities, vocations, countries and churches; consequently, the hard-won understanding of multiple perspectives came across clearly in interviews. Latinx leaders possess the skillsets and sensitivity to comprehend others and to nurture the development of their colleagues around them. But it is not enough to only understand other cultures and contexts; it is equally necessary to value the distinctives of others and to respect their way

78. Tomás.

79. Lingenfelter, Leading Cross-Culturally, 21.

of doing things. This is the complexity that contributes to learning.[80] Yanisa declared that Latinx leaders in CHE had to be multidimensional in their approach to serving others:

> We have to understand White culture or majority culture [because] we live in it. And I think if we don't understand that we will not be successful, so we have to know that culture. We also have to have the multicultural skills to understand domestic diversity; not that you have to be an expert on that . . . but being in a learner's stance. learning about other cultures, looking at data . . . figuring out how best to serve all of our students. And then intercultural again, with that international focus . . . thinking through what does it mean going out in the world, to be aware of the world and what's happening there . . . So I think all of that is about learning and modeling those skill sets to have an open mind to new ideas and to new ways of being, while still obviously staying true to the core, and so for me that means you've done your own work.
>
> I think we need to be aware that we ourselves carry bias, not just for White people at times, but also for others . . . We all do that . . . we are first world people and we need to have some openness to second and third world cultures . . . all of that . . . so we have to model that I think, because we're not in the driver's seat . . . White men don't have to although they should. I think that's what they're feeling this pushback about . . . for them it's like this threat that they're not in control anymore. Well, for [Latinx] they already know they're not in control, we've never been in the seat of power. So being the president of the university or being an executive, you have to be aware of how to bring others along by having these [intercultural] skill sets.[81]

Yanisa's descriptions of leading multiculturally provide a wealth of information on Latinx leading and serving in CHE. She specified that Latinx had to learn White culture and understand all the particulars of the context, while also learning domestic and international diversity to be fully versed in interculturality. Participants all felt that they brought this social and cultural capital since they have navigated these complexities all their lives and were bilingual, so it was natural for them.

Understanding power dynamics is also crucial for Latinx in CHE. Yanisa stated that Latinx have never been in full control and alluded to how White males have always been in these positions of power, so they assume

80. Lingenfelter and Lingenfelter, *Teaching Cross-Culturally*, 17.

81. Yanisa.

these influential roles. But Latinx, and women in particular, have to navigate the intersectionality of several worlds. A crucial practice that Yanisa identified was code-switching. When asked about her way of leading and serving in CHE, Yanisa declared:

> I grew up Pentecostal and in the Assemblies of God. But I have come a bit further towards grace and more to the teachings of the Mennonites and Quakers, about social justice and living out our faith in actual practice. I hope that I would marry the two together; the missional incarnation and the move of the Holy Spirit in my own life. By that I mean I can feel the Holy Spirit; I can hear the Spirit moving. But I have also coupled that with real strong action that comes from the Mennonite faith. . .so by that I mean it's both; horizontal and vertical. That is what drives me. What are some of the concerns about the Pentecostal spiritual? Some say it's too much. I call it code-switch. We do that . . . people of color code-switch; we switch words that will help us in certain communities.[82]

Yanisa attends a predominately White nondenominational church. She stressed that the Holy Spirit's movement was not as evident as it was in the churches in which she grew up. And although she does not feel comfortable to speak Holy Spirit language in her church, she does speak freely by code-switching language to the majority culture. "It may seem false but it's not." Yanisa defined code-switching as using the terminology that fits the situation or the group that is being addressed. Yanisa carried this practice over in CHE as an executive leader. The apostle Paul spoke comparably about being contextual (code-switching) when he declared:

> Though I am free and belong to no one, I have made myself a slave to everyone, to win as many as possible. To the Jews I became like a Jew, to win the Jews. To those under the law I became like one under the law (though I myself am not under the law), so as to win those under the law. To those not having the law I became like one not having the law (though I am not free from God's law but am under Christ's law), so as to win those not having the law. To the weak I became weak, to win the weak. I have become all things to all people so that by all possible means I might save some. I do all this for the sake of the gospel, that I may share in its blessings (1 Cor 9:1923, NIV).

Latinas interviewed seem to have learned methods of adapting to their environment in order to be effective in their leadership. Although most of them

---

82. Yanisa.

hold various perspectives different from those held by their institutions, for the most part they "code-switched" in order to be heard, to have influence, to get the job done and to reach their goals. Marisol stated that being a multicultural leader comes from listening and reflecting with others:

> The reflective piece is very important because becoming multicultural is a lifetime discipline. It's a discipline of faith . . . it's not a strategy. So for example, I have males, females, I have Puerto Rican, I have African American, I have Indian, I have White and Asians who are in my faculty . . . I have African . . . And what it takes for us to make this happen together is we all focus on our mission. And we understand that every day we see miracles because when a person is transformed a miracle takes place. A miracle is taking place, and I mean like really, a miracle is taking place.[83]

Participants frequently mentioned their ability to leverage others on their team through brainstorming and collaborative efforts. Latinx leaders' ability to blend in and move in-between cultures gives them the flexibility and access necessary to move the mission forward. They also talked about how domestic diversity and international diversity are important. The global mindset of Latinx leaders is impressive.

In today's global and interconnected society, change is normative for every organization. CHE operates in this context and will need to prepare students to work and serve in this multifaceted environment. But how will the CCCU and its institutions perform this service if most of its faculty and leadership are White? Chen and Starosta articulate a way forward:

> As we move toward multiculturalism and globalization it is not only the business world that must adapt to changes, the academic sector must deal with the trend as well. In the classroom, the necessity to accommodate cultural diversity is becoming more apparent. Education not only helps new immigrants to make sense of the local culture, it offers individuals insights and skills they need to survive in the changing world. Only through multicultural and global education can people learn about those problems and issues that cut across ethnic, national, and gender boundaries and learn to understand how other groups process experience in ways that may differ from our own perceptions.[84]

---

83. Marisol.

84. Chen and Starosta, Foundations of Intercultural Communication, 225.

Finally, Latinx leaders exhibit multiple essential traits of global leaders. According to Mark Mendenhall, "global leadership is the processes and actions through which an individual influences a range of internal and external constituents from multiple national cultures and jurisdictions in a context characterized by significant levels of task and relationship complexity."[85] Latinx leaders, as described above by Tomás and Yanisa, are able to adapt to their context and effectively serve and lead for a desired outcome.

According to the interviewees, along with knowing what battles leaders must pick and choose, Latinx leaders have to be adaptable in order to serve effectively in CHE. This is what Tomás stated when asked about sharing further:

> It's an isolated space for people of color in administration in particular. It's an isolated space in general when people of color in predominantly White institutions [are] trying to do the work of an evangelist of sorts in that space. You still got to play the chameleon role from a leadership perspective and integrating yourself in multiple spaces . . . .you have to be fluid . . . .you almost get caught [up] trying to be all things to all people in order to ensure that you're seen as effective, creative and [as] an innovator.[86]

Several essential leadership traits are clear from the Latinx interviewed, including adaptability, contextualization, and the ability to code-switch. In missional terms, Latinx leaders attributed excellence to the concept of contextual leadership.

Contextual Intelligence and Leadership

In the previous section of this chapter, the leadership frameworks that drive Latinx leaders were examined. In this section, the concept of contextual leadership will be expanded to put the concepts of chameleon, code-switching, and adaptability in conversation with the theology and contextualization of leaders' faith through service. This is known as contextual intelligence, or contextual leadership.

Latinx leaders have had to learn the CCCU context well enough to navigate its complexity, but the CCCU has not been required to learn about Latinx in general (at least not to the extent that Latinas have had to learn the CCCU and Whiteness). Although the Latinx leaders never described their leadership using the term "contextual intelligence," their descriptions

---

85. Mendenhall, Global Leadership, 23.

86. Tomás.

of their lived leadership experience correlate helpfully with this specific theory. Contextual intelligence or leadership gives substance to what these leaders have expressed: mainly, that Latinas need to possess the ability to move in and out of cultures, serve broadly, speak multiple languages, adjust, adapt, remain nimble and flexible enough to read and serve effectively in and out of their context.

The Latinx leaders interviewed demonstrated many characteristics and traits of contextual leaders. These leaders are adaptable and nimble. They exegete their environment and take the apostle Paul's council of making themselves "all things to all people." As several of them stated, they do not lose themselves in this endeavor, but they evolve and develop the skills necessary to be effective for their organization and the mission that they set out to achieve. This is a leadership concept that needs further investigation and research, but the Latinx leaders demonstrate this approach to leadership which has proven successful in CHE.

As previously mentioned, the contextualization dialogue that has historically permeated the West, its theological institutions and the church has primarily been related to anthropological or social-cultural analysis. On the other hand, Matthew Kutz developed a contextual intelligence model, meaning "to be aware of the different variables that are being brought to a situation and then accurately discern between alternate courses of action to select the best action and then execute it."[87] Kutz further writes that leaders will need to embrace 3D Thinking (three dimensional thinking) through hindsight, insight and foresight, which would give them a more accurate understanding of what was, what is, and what can be. And finally, contextual intelligence involves leveraging learning, reframing experience, and embracing complexity, which means diagnosing one's surroundings to better assess the context that would influence leaders' behaviors and those in relation to them.[88] Marisol, Tomás, Yanisa, Ruth, and Josue all personified this contextual leadership through their interviews.

The participants exemplified contextual leadership qualities that allowed them to have success in a culture that is not their own—specifically, White culture in CHE. They became "all things to all people" in order to maximize their efforts and fulfill the mission of their schools. Enduring a multitude of challenges as leaders of color, the Latinx executives demonstrated that they are relentless, contextual, and determined. Utilizing strategies such as embodying code-switching, communicating fluidly and

---

87. Kutz, Contextual Intelligence, 16. Please refer to Chapter Two for more information on Contextual Intelligence.

88. Kutz, Contextual Intelligence, 10.

broadly across gender lines or culture; engaging chameleon leadership in which Latinx exegeted the situation and then became whatever was needed; and employing contextual leadership, combining in practice the concepts of code-switching and chameleon—these and other leadership strategies were deployed in order to maximize effectiveness in the CCCU context. The Latinx leaders essentially found a way to lead and serve, no matter the circumstance.

All the executive Latinx leaders that were interviewed had diverse but similar experiences in CHE. Some of the positive experiences that Latinx leaders described included a profound sense of calling, the opportunity to make a positive difference, representing students and the Latinx community, and participating in God's plan for their schools. In contrast, all experienced racism, discrimination, microaggressions, and the pervasive notion of not being "mission fit." Likewise, all Latinx leaders felt that their institutions did not take diversity matters seriously enough, which was demonstrated by a lack of accountability, appropriate budgets, and the leadership support for the work of diversity, equity, and inclusion (DEI).

Interviewees acknowledged that their institutions usually had excuses for the lack of Latinx representation (and people of color) in the faculty and administrative ranks. Some of these excuses included perceptions that people of color have no interest in moving to more remote locations, and the perception that there were not enough competent applicants for a position. But the experiences of Latinx leaders interviewed indicates that this is incorrect.

When it came to faith and theological expressions, Latinx leaders' experiences in CHE are varied since their theology and missiology is just as diverse as their experiences in leadership. One thing is for certain: Latinx theology is not private, but rests on the *practica* (praxis) of seeing the oppressed and voiceless liberated.[89] The Eurocentric Jesus of the majority culture is focused on orthodoxy, but the *Jesús* of Latinas focuses on orthopraxis.[90] De La Torre asserts, "*Jesús* becomes present in the here and now, and, in fact, a lack of praxis signals a lack of faith because *Jesús* linked praxis to Salvation."[91] These ideas were expressed by the theological views of the interviewees, especially their inclination to promote faith through transformational justice and changes in educational practices.

For the participants, this theology is done solely by the work of the Holy Spirit. For Latinas, the work and movement of the Holy Spirit is

89. Rodríguez and Martell-Ortero, Teologia En Conjunto, 148.

90. De La Torre, Politics of Jesús, 52.

91. De La Torre, Politics of Jesús, 53.

tantamount for any liberation to be exercised.[92] The Holy Spirit is the one "who guides, empowers, and transforms,"[93] and the particpants were in agreement that nothing could be done without the support and guidance of the Spirit of God. The Latinx community will have to continue to address the issues of oppression within their theological praxis and leadership. One thing is certain: this theological reflection will not be done by one community alone somewhere in the Bronx, Los Angeles, Chicago, or even Texas. Loida I. Martell-Otero states that "this will have to be an orthopraxis reflection carried out *en conjunto* (together) within the U.S. Hispanic community of faith."[94] The Latinx that were interviewed demonstrated that they both led and served through collaboration and community.

U.S. Latinas are unique in their *practica* in terms of keeping the traditions of the past, but also extending their vision into the renewal of the future. Martell-Ortero claims, "this is the *adobo* (seasoning), the *sofrito* (herbs and spices), that gives *sabor* (flavor) to our theology, and which imbues us with the passion of our faith."[95] Latinx leaders in the CCCU hold promise for understanding the diverse theologies of the future student populations that await the work of CHE. And if Latinx leaders do not already understand these incoming diversities, they will learn them as Josue did, in order to understand students, the context, and the community much better. DEI are a part of the Latinx community, and according to Josue, as Latinx leaders begin to position themselves in the ranks of the administration in the CCCU, these institutions of higher education will be strategically positioned to understand and serve the reign of God more broadly.

The future of the Latina church in the U.S. looks very promising.[96] However, even though the Latinx church continues to see growth, it is not clear what the future holds for her leaders within CHE. Although the fastest-growing student population is Latina, there are no signs that Latinx leaders are growing at the pace of students in the administration ranks of the CCCU, or any signs of intentionality to create pipelines for such leaders.[97] At the time of concluding this book, only one of the five Latinx leaders

92. Rodríguez and Martell-Ortero, Teologia En Conjunto, 148.

93. Rodríguez and Martell-Ortero, Teologia En Conjunto, 148.

94. Rodríguez and Martell-Ortero, Teologia En Conjunto, 148.

95. Rodríguez and Martell-Ortero, Teologia En Conjunto, 149.

96. Martínez, Story of Latino Protestants, 202.

97. CCCU, Diversity Matters, 121–122, showcases Latinx administration (fulltime and part time) having minor growth of 1.9 percent from 2007–08 to 2017–18. As Ruth stated, "And who is asking the institutions to create the pipeline and equipping them to make sure that they are diverse? We have been talking about the pockets forever in terms of faculty representation and the diversity there; in terms of student population

interviewed remains in the CCCU. No one can predict the future with confidence, but one thing is for certain: the CCCU needs to change in order to survive the demographic shifts and educational trends that await her within the U.S.

The Latinx leaders interviewed all demonstrated some common traits in their leadership, including being service-oriented (servant leadership), adaptability (flexibility), chameleon-type (able to conform to an environment without losing oneself), and most importantly, contextual (a deep understanding of their surroundings, inclusive of political, social-cultural, economic and religious aspects). Latinas lead from a relational standpoint. Marisol was very resolute about the necessity of leading for the benefit of the people, if one desires to serve in CHE. This relational component, in this researcher's observation, comes from a profound relationship with Jesus. These Latinx leaders are full of God and lead from a place of humility, respect, love and selflessness.

What does this all mean for Latinx leaders in CHE, and the CCCU overall? The next and final chapter addresses these questions by providing recommendations and suggestions for Latinx leaders and CHE.

---

and the diversity there; in terms of administration even at the level of presidents. There are huge gaps that exist. We have taken steps towards the right direction, but at the pace that we are going, are we really going to experience it?"

5

The Promise of Latinx Leaders: A Call to Christian Higher Education

It is time for a reckoning, for Christian Higher Education (CHE) and for the United States as a whole. Latinx leaders are ready to serve. They are missional, flexible, and perfectly equipped and prepared to navigate the changing racial and ethnic face of the U.S. in the coming decades. But if CHE is more profoundly wedded to cultural Whiteness than to Jesus, continuing to overlook these promising Latinx and other leaders of color and to promote those persons of privilege who have held power since the beginning, I fear that CHE will miss the provision of God and languish.

In this research process, I set out to investigate and understand the experiences of executive Latinx leaders in CHE, specifically those that serve in the Council of Christian Colleges and Universities (CCCU). I did this by examining their experiences using Critical Race Theory (CRT) and Latina/o Critical Race Theory (LatCrit). The questions I asked these leaders were:

1. What are the experiences of executive Latinx administrators at CCCU schools?

2. What theological and missiological frameworks drive Latinx leaders in Christian higher education?

3. What type of leadership is needed by Latinx leaders to succeed in Christian higher education?

4. Is there anything else that you may want to add to this project that you may have left out?

5. Is there anything from current events that you think or feel applies to diversity, equity, and inclusion as it pertains to Christian higher education?

I analyzed the data collected in several ways: (1) showcased the participants' answers by using CRT and LatCrit and presented the findings in a general format so that the reader could make sense of what the Latinx leaders stated; (2) categorized themes from all the interviews and put them within the first three main questions' blocks; that is, experiences, theology and missiology, and leadership,[1] and (3) in this chapter, presented the findings of what was originally discovered in order to make sense of it for future use.

THEMES AND FINDINGS

From the interviews, nine themes emerged. These themes are:

1. Systemic racism experienced by Latinx

2. The notion of Whiteness and mission fit

3. The glass ceiling

4. Justice and faith

5. Prayer and total dependence on the Holy Spirit

6. Collaborative and community-driven leadership

7. Lifelong learners

8. Chameleon and code-switching leadership

9. Contextual Intelligence and leadership

I will classify these themes below under the three main categories taken from the initial questions: (I) experiences, (II) theology and missiology, and (III) leadership—allowing for practical organization of the data.

---

1. Although there were five main block questions, I filed all the answers under the first three main block questions since it made the findings simpler and cleaner for the reader to understand.

WHAT ARE THE EXPERIENCES OF
EXECUTIVE LATINX LEADERS?

One of the main themes that emerged when the Latinx leaders were asked about their experiences in the CCCU was systemic racism. This means that all the participants felt that they were discriminated against in one way or another, although Josue mentioned he did not think he had as much difficulty on this front as his colleagues did, since he "did not inherit his father's dark skin color." Nevertheless, Tomás declared that he experienced "direct oppression" from board members and other senior leaders, while Ruth concurred with him about oppression and added "there is institutional racism." These leaders were clear that the organization of Christian higher education (CHE) was not created with them in mind, but catered to the majority culture.

All participants, in one way or another, stated that they experienced microaggressions and felt excluded at times. And while the work of an executive leader is already a difficult task, they had to fight against culturally illiterate people, systems, and policies that made their job problematic. Sometimes being Latinx was a challenge, according to the participants, since they did not know if their identity would be taken well, or if they would be facing prejudice and unconscious bias.

According to the participants, the lack of accountability in CCCU schools and the lack of budgets to get tangible work done in diversity efforts is a significant deficit. According to Ruth, "There is a huge lack to be able to hold accountable and to have institutions to serve in the role of advocacy, to help institutions that are bound by the stronghold of institutional racism." In other words, there is not enough accountability from the top with board members because they are just as deficient in diversity. Therefore, there is no advocacy, so systemic racism continues to perpetuate itself.

Based on the accounts shared by the Latinx leaders, CHE would benefit from rethinking how business is conducted. In other words, a restructuring of some sort is indicated, in which policies create operational accountability among the board members, the presidents, and the cabinet executive members. Unless there are repercussions for certain actions or non-actions, how will things ever change? We remember here Tomás' suggestion that real change will come when presidents risk being fired if they fail to address deficiencies in diversity in their institutions. Unless presidents—and board members, for that matter—are accountable for this work, things will continue to stay as they have always been.

Other questions to lead to improvement might include: first, how are board members chosen and with what agenda are they presented so that expectations are clearly identified, and key metrics reviewed annually? Are board leaders creating or given a map of where the institution wants to be in five or ten years on these DEI matters? As the research has demonstrated, diversity starts with the top executive leadership, including the board of trustees, the president and cabinet, the provost, and academic leadership teams. Secondly, are presidents hired and given the charge to DEI with the same intensity and emphasis as they are charged with fundraising, increasing enrollments, and branding the school? These are the types of metrics and emphases that would help a traditional university move the pendulum of change for a more inclusive campus. The issue here, as we have seen, is that DEI work overall is a second-rate desire, with most efforts in this direction lacking the funding or emphasis that would lead to progress.

Thirdly, accountability should not only be required of the board, the president, and the cabinet, but also of deans, academic teams, and staff members. The tenure process must have DEI efforts embedded in it. In other words, if faculty want to work at an institution, they will need to include diverse voices in the core curriculum, target program learning outcomes that enable students and faculty to learn together about national and global diversity, and host conversations that, although they may be uncomfortable, are needed to push the DEI agenda forward within the educational setting. Provosts need to be diversity champions who are competent in DEI and who see their position as an ambassador for the academic community. How will faculty be accountable if the provost does not hold them accountable? This also requires new policies that enable this work to be carried out throughout academic affairs; therefore, a task force or longstanding committee would need to be established by the provost's office that is charged with setting the pace for strategic leadership change as it relates to DEI.

Fourth, staff should be engaged at every level, since they have their ears to the ground and are generally involved with all the operations of the university. Staff need to be on task force or committee assignments, speaking into issues of the workplace and culture of the organization; a strategic partnership with human resources is an imperative. They should also have input on the day-to-day activities related to DEI, and they can add value by pointing out academic or leadership blind spots. And finally, students need to be involved at every level. Students can be brought into the board meetings and invited to speak about gaps and discrepancies that they have experienced on campus. Students can speak to curriculum that they think is needed, lacking, or can be strengthened by faculty. In other words, end-of-course surveys should include questions that ask directly about the cultural and inclusion aspects of the subject matter and classroom. Also, it is imperative for students to be asked to provide feedback about the professor's approach in class, their intercultural competence, and their sensitivity to global citizenship. Students are one of the main shareholder populations, especially in tuition-driven institutions, and they should be involved in decision-making. For overall accountability, I am asking CHE schools to think through what Josue stated about the need to reframe the entire institution. CCCU schools were created with the majority culture in mind. However, we are experiencing drastic demographic, socioeconomic, and technological changes that will need strategic planning and foresight for the twenty first century.

WHITENESS AND MISSION FIT

Whiteness and mission fit were another clustered theme that the Latinx clearly articulated contributing to the divisive predisposition to marginalize Latinx in Christian higher education (CHE).[2] The inclination to second-guess Latinx and their presence, along with their competence in the senior ranks of their schools, was an experiential burden that all interviewees shared. Tomás clearly stated that board members at his institution expressed astonishment when they found out that he was the senior academic leader on campus. From his perspective, this astonishment simply resulted because he was a person of color.

Yanisa was adamant about the ways in which systemic racism is interwoven in the fabric of U.S. society and how it replicates itself smoothly

---

2. White hegemony, according to Collins and Jun, is "cultural power, including the dominant cultural patterns that achieve and sustain their dominance by encouraging—but not forcing—people to believe in them" (Collins and Jun, White Out, 100). Hegemonic Whiteness is an identity that both produces and maintains domination through power and privilege. Whiteness is internalized as normal and natural, in turn marking non-Whites as abnormal and unnatural. Dominance and subordination thus are sustained, not necessarily by force, but through social practices, systems, and norms. Systems of oppression are maintained because society does not challenge the validity of norms and attitudes that perpetuate systems of domination and subordination because they are viewed as normal.

Mission fit can be discerned from the following: "Particularly in religiously-affiliated institutions, denominational preferences could be barriers for those individuals who desire to work at colleges or universities that are affiliated with a church denomination. To ascend to certain levels of leadership, it is not uncommon for some religiously-affiliated institutions to ask candidates vying for executive level positions if they would be willing to switch their church affiliation. In some cases, it is required that all senior level leaders join a church denomination affiliated with their institution. For administrators of color, the barriers could be interpreted as a way for the dominant culture to maintain the balance of power and limit access to underrepresented individuals who are both qualified and competent to successfully lead" (Moffit, "A Narrative Study," 24).

in CHE. More specifically, Whiteness was a norm important enough that if Latinx would not assimilate to it, they would soon find themselves either out of a job or marginalized further. In other words, Whiteness is the ordinary standard of the university, and mission fit is code for whether or not a Latinx could conform to those expectations of fitting in with majority culture philosophy. Anything outside of this coded Whiteness would be considered abnormal and out of order. The constant discernment challenge that Latinx leaders face here is whether it is time to assimilate to White normativity in order to get the job done and have some sense of belonging, versus whether it is time to stand up or call out something as a deal-breaker for them due to their ethics, convictions, and their sense of calling.

Upholding Whiteness plays into the "mission fit" doctrine of an institution, according to the Latinx participants. Said differently, Whiteness is the normative standard or culture of the university, and mission fit is whether or not a Latinx could assimilate to those expectations of fitting in with majority culture ethos.[3] All participants stated that unless you were considered a "good fit," which really meant ascribing to White normativity, you would not be given a job. Search committees and faculty and administrative searches are doomed from the beginning with diversity lacking on the committee, and no one present who can mitigate bias and favoritism.

This is an area of opportunity for the CCCU, as it pertains to malleable processes and protocols by which employment searches are conducted. For example, a policy can be created from the president's and provost's offices clearly articulating that search committees need a variety of people on them from different schools, disciplines, and cultural backgrounds. A chief diversity officer (CDO) or other expert on implicit bias should sit on upper-level searches, while search firms or consultants can be employed from the outside to help an institution diversify its portfolio and search methods. Excuses such as "there aren't any good or qualified applicants," or "people of color do not want to move here," or "we just don't know anyone who would be interested in this position," should always be challenged. Final candidates for all searches should be rejected if women and diversity are not represented. Building institutional capacity for DEI is a multidimensional effort that will take the intentionality and commitment of multiple stakeholders, along with strategic relationship building.[4]

The Latinx participants explained that being or not being "mission fit" was a strategy or unspoken practice that was used to keep people of color out of Predominately White Institutions (PWIs). Whether done intentionally or

3. See Chapter 4, Testimonios.
4. Smith, Diversity's Promise, 282–283.

not, this system of discrimination continues to replicate itself in CHE. One way that White privilege and mission fit preserve themselves in the CCCU is via the silence surrounding these issues. Marisol declared:

> I have been in different settings and each setting is different. I have found that in liberal settings you still deal with the racism and so forth, but you are able to have conversations about it much more readily than in evangelical circles. Evangelical circles believe that they are converted so they don't have to deal with the Black and White box, or much less the Latino box.[5]

White theology assumes and operates as if it is neutral and objective, but it is just like other theologies: subjective and contextual.[6] Participants interviewed felt that White colleagues needed to deal with their blinders in order for CHE to become more diverse and inclusive.

Challenging the notion that "we are not racist" should not be a problem if, in fact, the institution is not racist. To find out, CCCU schools can facilitate conversations in the community by reading a book together that grapples with Whiteness, male privilege, colorblindness, equity, inclusion, and belonging, or majority and minority relations. This can open intercultural communication lines and help community members learn and understand the school's present cultural climate without relying on assumptions. An expert like a CDO could facilitate these rich conversations. The point here is that the tendencies to shy away from tough conversations or to assume that diversity issues do not exist on campus should be contested, in order to create a safe campus and a sense of belonging for everyone.

U.S. society is facing much social unrest as problems including police violence and hate crimes continue to escalate, as people take advantage of peaceful protests by vandalizing property, and as polarized politics persist. CCCU schools can see this time of unrest as an opportunity to be "salt and light" (as well as part of the solution), refusing the temptation to be complicit by silence. Communities of color are hurting and the Latinx leaders interviewed confirmed the suffering experienced in CCCU schools. In Christian communities of justice, compassion and equality, we are all needed for human flourishing. This is an opportune time for transformational change.

---

5. Marisol.

6. For more on White Theology, White Jesus, and Whiteness in general, see Collins and Jun, White Out, Jun et al; White Jesus, Jennings, The Christian Imagination; Romero, Brown Church; and De La Torre, Decolonizing Christianity and The Politics of Jesús; all referenced elsewhere in this book.

THE GLASS CEILING

All but one of the Latinx participants asserted that there was a real issue with the "glass ceiling," in terms of women having an equitable chance at executive leadership roles. While there has been some growth in the CCCU presidential office in terms of women, which should not be minimized, all of the recent appointments as of this writing have been White women. Common knowledge is that Affirmative Action has helped White women the most, which seems to have played itself out within the CCCU.[7]

It is interesting to note that the majority of the global church is female, yet this ecclesial body is governed primarily by men. The same is true for CHE. The majority of students are women, but the leadership roles are dominated by White men.[8] This seems like a good time to begin to transition from a male-privileged and White male-dominant leadership to an equitable community, encompassing all people.

Marisol, Ruth, and Yanisa all stressed the fact that women have to be very careful to not be labeled "too emotional" or other feminine stereotypes that hinder the progress of executive Latinx leaders. They stated that men get many breaks and can let some steam off, but women have to be very professional at all times. According to Marisol, Ruth, and Yanisa, there exists a double standard for leadership when it comes to men and women in CHE, which further contributes to sexism and marginalization. Tomás stated that he was an ally for women in leadership and carried that out in his own leadership service. This is something that all men can do to help CHE become more diverse and inclusive, and to open the pathway for equity across gender lines. The inclusion of more women in leadership can also be achieved through accountability, new policies, and educating campuses on broader leadership issues. Again, searches should be launched with women in mind through metrics attainable. CCCU schools can no longer use the excuse that there are not enough women leaders available, since there are many highly qualified women who are ready to assume executive leadership positions within CHE.

THEOLOGICAL AND MISSIOLOGICAL
FRAMEWORKS DRIVING LATINX LEADERS

Strong themes emerged while interviewing the Latinx leaders about their faith. The themes that emerged were justice and faith, prayer, and

---

7. Wise, "Is Sisterhood Conditional?," 1.

8. Longman and Anderson, "Women in Leadership," 24.

dependence on the Holy Spirit. All participants expressed their view of faith as it pertained to justice. In other words, their faith (their understanding of theology and missiology) propelled them to act publicly, and not to hold a merely private faith.

For example, when Tomás was asked about his theological and missiological views related to Christian higher education, he stated "I lean towards the oppressed, the marginalized, and the poor." In other words, he purposefully served those who were considered the least within the community. Marisol also expanded this thought by asserting, "Christian higher education began as a way of addressing issues of justice. That's how it began. Giving people access to education. Helping people get jobs. Teaching the children of immigrants. The evangelical church was a part of all of that." Latinx leaders considered their work in CHE a ministry of justice and equity. They saw themselves as leaders called by God to be light and make a transformational difference in the lives of the people they were serving.

The Latinx leaders interviewed did not see their own faith in a vacuum or interpret it as being simply about correct doctrine. They saw and expressed a missiology that was concerned with the current society and CHE. They did not explain their faith as something that separates the sacred and the secular, but a way of living that impacted all aspects of their lives, including work, society, and family.

Justice work, according to participants, is getting involved where there are injustices. They called for the CCCU and the church to be intentional about getting involved with justice. Josue stated: "I think the call for true justice . . . we needed and need to be at the vanguard of those discussions instead of being at the trailer . . . we need to be at the forefront of that. The heart of Jesus was to go to the Samaritan woman and that's not where we have been, we just haven't . . . and part of it for me is intentionality." Josue was clear that the CCCU is not at the forefront of justice and equity conversations; nor is it doing the actual work of inclusion and equity.

All the participants felt that the CCCU could do more in terms of DEI. No one expressed contentment with the current climate of the CCCU, nor did anyone think or express that their institution was doing the work of justice completely. In other words, all participants declared that there was more work to be done and that the CCCU was actually lagging behind secular institutions like the NBA and the NFL. This is sad to hear, since CHE is a place that represents the community of God and prepares Christian leaders for work and ministry. Yet, at least according to these interviews, it seems like we are the ones who continue to perpetuate racism and bias towards one another.

Yanisa explained that justice work can feel exhausting and that she had learned to lean more on God. This is a very significant point for Latinx and people of color reading this book. Yanisa said, "you can literally die if you don't take care of yourself." Hence, she is calling all people of color to prioritize rest and to take all their burdens to God by prayer and fasting.

Ruth was very resolute about praying for everything. She stated that it was impossible to be in this work without this kind of constant prayer. The *waiting* that all Latinx felt in the CCCU was telling. They all felt that the CCCU has been very slow to address systemic racism and all the issues that come from it. Therefore, a life of prayer was imperative to give the leader resources to endure the sluggish responses to inequities. Ruth was clear that we would not ever see real change at the current pace CHE was moving.

The participants were adamant that a life of prayer was important in this faith journey and for those serving in CHE particularly. They spoke of being in deep intimacy with the Holy Spirit as a way to not only endure the struggles of the CCCU, but also for the ability to be used as a change agent in CHE. They spoke about seeing things as God sees them. Ruth declared, "Everything is different when you see it from the lenses of God." Their hope was that their White colleagues in the CCCU would also embody this revelation of faith and allow the Holy Spirit to work in them in ways that would stretch them to work and advocate further for DEI.

The participants stated that they grew up praying and believing in God because they needed to. Tomás professed: "When I think of spiritual formation, I think to the degree to how I can experience God through discipleship and prayer, scripture reading and streams of freshness, holiness, and justice." There is an expectation from the Latinx leaders that if a person "presses in" to get to know God, then it is possible to actually know God more. In other words, knowing God personally was an expectation for the Latinx leaders. They brought these expectations and experiences to their work. Experiencing miracles was also common in the spiritual experience of these Latinx leaders, and they embodied this in their leadership roles in CHE. They did not put limits on God, and they led and served with this in mind.

Latinx leaders stated that they prayed and confided in the Holy Spirit for everything. Tomás' comment about "walking on his knees" still echoes in my ears, illustrating how dependent these Latinx leaders are on divine guidance and leadership. Ruth stated that her theology was formed from witnessing miracles growing up, praying for hours for provision, and not stopping until those prayers were answered. This spiritual resilience is evident in the lives of these Latinx leaders and demonstrates how they can withstand much controversy and conflict within the CCCU. This also shows why they endure so much discrimination and maltreatment: they truly believe that the situation can change.

The greatest attribute of these Latinx leaders' faith is that they see their ministry in CHE as working first for God. They advocate for justice because they believe that this is what God wants them to do. They pray and live a life of holiness, expecting to experience God at work, because they believe that the Lord is actually present and active in their work. Josue expressed that he experienced significant hurt and pain in CHE, but that he knew that he was right where he was supposed to be. In other words, the Latinx leaders were in CHE because of their call to serve God in justice through their faith, empowered by the Holy Spirit.

The CCCU can grow in its diversity of theology and missiology by inviting faculty of color to create courses that expose students to the variety of beliefs that exist. This can be accomplished by allowing such courses to be situated in the core curriculum, and faculty can be given a course reduction of some fashion in order to complete this project. Another option would be to hire or contract faculty from other institutions and bring them on as visiting faculty in order to expose the community to the richness and diversity of theologies that exist in world Christianity.

Lastly, concerning missiology, a nonwestern and postcolonial perspective needs to be presented to students. We do not want the next generation of leaders committing the same mistakes of the previous generation. A fresh look at what the *Missio Dei* looks like and how it is carried out would be highly beneficial. The study of missiology is taking some interesting turns and going through many innovations. Additionally, missiologists and other leaders from the Global South should be brought in to expose the campus community to some of the ways in which the Holy Spirit is moving around the world.

WHAT TYPE OF LEADERSHIP IS NEEDED BY LATINX LEADERS?

Several leadership themes emerged as I interviewed the participants. These are: valuing collaborative and community-driven leadership, being lifelong learners, chameleon and code-switching leadership, and contextual intelligence and leadership.

The Latinx interviewed all lead from a place of relationships, and each one believes that building community is crucial. They described this as an incarnational way of serving and leading in the CCCU. They tried to connect authentically with people and get to know them personally. Latinx leaders believe that leading from relationships was more effective than leading from their position. This made sense since most of these leaders described feeling doubted or "suspect" in their positions at times, so having deep relationships with colleagues would go a long way.

Marisol stated that Latinx leaders needed to ask questions and really listen to others; this was the only way to figure out others' needs. Deep conversations and dialogue are the approaches that can give leaders insight into the school, the community, and their colleagues. The participants explained that learning was a key to their success. Leadership, as described by the participants, was a journey and should be seen as such. Latinx leaders worked on listening, asking many questions, and taking the time to get familiar with everyone they encountered in their place of work and service.

Tomás and other participants explained that they could do such things well because they were like chameleons: in other words, able to adapt well to varied environments. I suspect that this is one of the main factors for success in the CCCU for Latinx: the ability to adapt, stay flexible, and blend with one's environment without losing one's identity—Latinx. Latinx will have to be comfortable adapting to various situations to effectively lead and serve their institutions.

For chameleon leaders, there are certain behaviors that unfold—adaptability, flexibility, and the willingness to maximize learning about one's own surroundings. However, Latinx leaders also spoke of code-switching to have success in CHE. Yanisa spoke specifically about having to learn to speak multiple languages, whether this pertained to awareness of white male norms, or altering the volume of one's voice, even the tone of how someone communicates: all these are part of code-switching. Learning and knowing well the audience and how to express oneself accordingly was a key to these diverse communication features.

Highly relevant to and descriptive of Latinx leadership is the concept of Contextual Intelligence, which according to Matthew Kutz is "to be aware of the different variables that are being brought to a situation and then accurately discern between alternate courses of action to select the best action and then execute it."[9] Kutz also described 3D Thinking (three-dimensional thinking) through hindsight, insight, and foresight, which would give leaders a more accurate understanding of what was, what is, and what can or will be. Additionally, contextual intelligence requires leveraging learning, reframing experience, and embracing complexity, which means diagnosing one's own context to better assess the needs of the environment.[10]

9. Kutz, Contextual Intelligence, 16.

10. Kutz, Contextual Intelligence, 10.

The Latinx leaders spoke of these concepts without naming them "contextual intelligence." But I observed that the connection of chameleon, code-switching and contextual intelligence exemplified by these leaders aligns well with the skill set and practices of contextual leadership. These leaders can join God in the *Missio Dei* and exegete their environmental needs, assessing the present situation and leading and serving from that point—rather than entering a situation with predisposed ideas or biases. Latinx demonstrate a contextual approach to leadership in that they allow the situation, context and or environment to speak to them and discern what needs exist, allowing them to provide the appropriate strategies in order to serve and empower others.

Developing contextual leaders in CHE will be a prominent next step for the CCCU in its attempts to become more diverse and inclusive. Students, faculty, staff, and administrators can be provided with experiences that take them out of their known environment, culture, or traditions. Being put in a position or place where you are not the majority can be very educational. Let me be clear: I am not referring to being a missionary in the historic sense and considering oneself a minority, while still holding structural power and having the ability to leave whenever one might choose. Rather, I am describing the experience of serving in a community where one does not have power, privilege, or influence. Being in this type of situation helps leaders to understand what it means to be in other people's shoes.

RECOMMENDATIONS FOR LATINX LEADERS

I asked the interviewees to identify three final pieces of advice they wanted to give to up-and-coming Latinx leaders in Christian higher education, since their experience and education has the potential to speak directly to the next generation of leaders and scholars. Tomás gave these three pieces of advice for up-and-coming Latinx leaders:

1. Understand who you are in the context of how God made you and who God made you to be. In other words, have a strong identity in Christ as a Latino (culture and faith). This needs to be solid as much as possible because challenges will come on one of those two fronts.

2. Ask as many questions as possible. Never believe that you are the first one or the only one. Ask and seek wisdom from those who have gone before you.

3. Make your own path. Follow your heart and dreams, build your own legacy, and be intentional. This is done with a great sense of orientation. You have to drive yourself to learning and stay grounded.

Marisol gave these three pieces of advice for up-and-coming Latinx leaders:

1. Be centered on Christ.

2. Make relationships what you are about, be creative, and be discerning of the spaces you choose. Have a purpose and a mission.

3. Don't let the agenda of privilege trump what the mission of the Spirit is for your life in this position.

Ruth gave these three pieces of advice for up-and-coming Latinx leaders:

1. Seek first the Kingdom of God and all things will be added to you. Be true to yourself. Embrace your *Latinidad*. God made you like this.

2. Find and surround yourself with people who will help you define who you are in Christ. Do not do it alone.

3. Speak up for your sisters and brothers. Be a voice. Speak up in the face of injustice and be a person who does not settle (there are things you will have to negotiate or conform to in order to have a seat at the table, but never sell out for it. You have to know what is nonnegotiable for you or what is totally against your ethics). Think about the next generation and let's make it better and easier for them.

Josue gave these three pieces of advice for up-and-coming Latinx leaders:

1. Make holiness your highest goal for the call God has called you. If you sacrifice your integrity, you will not achieve what you have set out to accomplish.

2. Pursue humility.

3. Be relentless in your goals. Never compromise and always be overprepared as much as you can. You want to be known as a person whose work is great and excellence is your priority. Never fall into complacency.

Yanisa gave these three pieces of advice for up-and-coming Latinx leaders:

1. Make sure you are following the calling that the Lord has given you.

2. Hold things loosely. While it's the call, get your emotional needs meet outside the job with family and church.

3. Understand that people are doing the best they can and treat them with grace. But also get things done. If someone is not the right person

for a job, move them. Sometimes you are not the right person in a job; therefore, acknowledge it. Always be excellent at what you do.

RECOMMENDATIONS FOR CHE

This book provides vital insights in pointing Latinx leaders and other people of color in the right direction for leading and navigating Predominately White Institutions (PWIs). Therefore, I thought it would be beneficial for the CCCU to also receive recommendations on how they could evolve, grow, and learn from the Latinx interviewed and from my own experience within CHE. The following are robust recommendations for CCCU schools, search committees and firms, presidents, and boards of trustees for various institutions of higher learning looking to recruit and retain Latinx administrators, women, and others underrepresented in these settings.

Listen to the Latinx You Have

One of the greatest frustrations the Latinx leaders communicated to me was the CCCU's inability or refusal to listen to Latinx and other people of color. This, of course, is contrary to public claims, since most CCCU schools would state that they want to become more diverse and inclusive; yet, they do not listen well to the limited but existing diversity that they have on campus. Listening to these voices would give the CCCU a competitive advantage since it would bring further awareness of where they currently stand in terms of diversity from internal consultants. Latinx voiced their disappointment that they are not considered a prophet in their own home. After listening, take steps to address strategic change to favor diversity, equity, and inclusion on the campus community. Ask those same leaders if they will assist in diversification programming or other plans that come out of such meetings. Some of these leaders may even take on additional responsibilities in these areas if they feel valued and expect that change will come out of their participation.

Create Pipelines for Latinx Leaders and Faculty

One justification for the lack of diversity often heard or communicated within the CCCU and CHE is that there just are not enough competent people of color or Latinx available. However, there are now many proficient people of color willing to take up the mantle of leadership in CHE, and even relocate if they must. It will be up to colleges and universities to create incentives for people of color to come and put up with the many inconveniences outlined in this book.

The other strategy that colleges and universities can incorporate is investing in their own pipeline of candidates from within. In other words, develop and groom your own leaders and faculty of color so that they have opportunities for advancement available to them. It only requires some foresight and strategic investments by the institution. CCCU schools will need to use their own networks and those outside the CCCU to recruit and retain viable Latinx for leadership positions. Administrators should also be considered for promotion and tenure based on their annual job performance related to diversity, equity, and inclusion (DEI). As the participants insisted, this needs to be valued highly enough to cost someone their job if they cannot commit to this work.

When it comes to faculty (although this research was mostly about administrators), the CCCU should consider hiring people of color (and women!) in clusters or groups so that they do not feel isolated on campus and have a greater chance to discover and build community in White spaces. This also is an investment and would support long-term success. These faculty should also have tenure so that they can have a long-lasting impact on the campus community and on culture, curriculum, systems, and polices on campus. Tenure also needs to be connected to faculty promotion and status. In other words, DEI should be an essential component of tenure processes at a Christian institution. These leaders need voice and voting privileges to create change.

Faculty are very important in this conversation since they are the keepers of knowledge on campus. Faculty are the ones who will need to introduce diverse voices to students and the community in classes and programs; they are the ones who have perhaps the greatest opportunity to host deeper discussions so that "diversity" might go beyond window dressing or tokenism. Faculty with research agendas in ethnic or gender studies, cultural studies, and other unconventional areas for the CCCU should be sought.

Diversify the Board of Trustees (BOT)

As we established earlier, diversity starts at the top of an institution. This means that the BOT will need to be diversified by race and ethnicity, gender and identity, ability and disability, generation, and areas of expertise. CCCU schools will have to go beyond their own graduates since most of these graduates are currently White. They will have to seek strategic donors who also value diversity, and they will have to discover people of color and women who have done the work of equity. There is no more excuse for not having people of color on the BOT with so many women CEO's and people of color now at the highest ranks of the marketplace. There are also many influential pastors of color who can serve themselves or recommend others from their networks.

If the BOT does not value or see the significance of a diversified school, it will be very difficult for the president and senior team to diversify. This must be a strategic team effort of leaders all moving in the same direction. The BOT will also need to make sure that the campus is setting a plan for diversity, equity, and inclusion, applying accountability to the plan, and setting goals and metrics to follow.

Hire a Chief Diversity Officer (CDO) and Vice President

Every college and university should hire a CDO and vice president of diversity, equity, and inclusion (DEI). This recommendation really should be the first step, since this person can help by serving as an internal change agent for the BOT, president and cabinet, leadership, faculty, and the rest of the community. This person needs to report to the president of the university and be a part of the executive leadership team. The CDO will need an adequate budget with their position, the influence and backing of the president and BOT, and support from the rest of the executive team to maximize the chances for success and positive impact as a collaborative leader.

The CDO and vice president need to be charged with creating a strategic DEI plan that spans the entire campus, from academics to enrollment, facilities, sports, marketing, and advancement efforts. Furthermore, this strategic plan should guide the campus on all its decisions, investments, and future trajectory.

An excellent CDO can help the campus create safe spaces for growth and belonging, providing through staff and team members training and awareness on unconscious bias, and helping search committees expand their reach for diverse hires. In other words, this vice president and CDO could lead the campus in a direction that would contribute to a more inclusive environment for all to thrive. This is the lead person that is hired to simply think on a daily basis about diversity and help the institution come along and serve towards that strategic purpose. The CDO would develop safe environments for courageous conversations and living, host conferences and seminars, address core curriculum with the provost and deans, and address diversity and help the institution reframe its entire formation of thinking and operating.

An example of this position and how it can make change comes from one of the Latinx that I interviewed—Yanisa. Yanisa is charged with leading all DEI efforts at her institution. While the other Latinx interviewed naturally must deal with diversity issues because of who they are and the extra responsibilities that they have accepted, part of Yanisa's position explicitly relates to diversity. She has enabled the university to rethink how they operate, how they address systemic racism, and how to move more towards inclusion and equity.

Yanisa shared in "the Jairus and the woman with the issue of blood" story how she would have to serve the one in power (White men), and those who are minoritized (people of color and women). She envisioned herself like a bridge, a connector of the community helping people make the connections with each other and their work. She would create spaces for conversations so that silos were not dividing people. She also asserted that she either sat on search committees or assigned someone to help in order to diminish unconscious bias.

Through my interviews with Yanisa, she shared that she had created a strategic diversity plan that encompassed the whole university and guided the work from the president's office. This plan served as a road map across academic affairs and other important departments on campus because it was created in collaboration with them. These teams and the work of the CDO have enabled the university to make progress towards a more inclusive and diverse community. And although Yanisa would be the first to state that they have a lot more progress to make, they have indeed made improvements because of their intentionality in addressing DEI. There exists no mystery to this work, only strong intentions and motivations, and placing someone in charge (with a strong budget and team) to generate progress in this area of service. The more people involved in the community the better off the diversity efforts become, since everyone takes full responsibility for the work.

Prayer and Fasting

CCCU schools should be very bold in inviting God to help them in this endeavor to diversify since this is God's agenda in the first place. CCCU schools are institutions of higher learning that have put faith front and center. The CCCU could advocate for a national week devoted to prayer and fasting, asking for the Holy Spirit to break the chains, traditions, and systems of racism. If we trust God for help, God will bring it and exceed our expectations. The Latinx leaders interviewed in this project testified over and over how they witnessed miracles from God. Prayer and fasting really should start from the BOT, president and executive team, engaging the faculty and students, creating a community-driven event for revival. God will change the hearts of everyone. We just need to ask; for is there anything impossible for God? (Luke 1:37)

Other Advice

A fuller understanding of mission is needed for the White evangelical church and, by extension, for CHE. No longer can we profess to have a personal relationship with Jesus and not act in love towards others. We cannot continue to be blind to the injustices borne by immigrants, children, women and other vulnerable populations. We cannot continue to perpetuate Whiteness in the name of the Gospel when it represents more truthfully the love of money and power. We can no longer tolerate so many deaths by guns in the U.S. only because its market provides funding for certain politicians. And our Kingdom of God citizenship needs to supersede our political affiliation on earth (Jesus is neither a Republican nor a Democrat!). We can no longer be silent about all the injustices we witness daily. No, we need, as Orlando Costas described, a Christ that is outside the gate that comes for all who are in-or-out of our groups. Jesus calls us to go and "share in his suffering by serving, especially, its lowest representative: the poor, the powerless, and the oppressed."[11]

What is needed in this century is a church that is as outward-focused as it is inward-looking. We need a powerful church that demonstrates its influence through love in both private and public sectors. Times have changed and more transformation is inevitable. As Amos Yong decrees:

> If we are ever to overcome the heresy of whiteness, the heterodoxy of European colonialism, and the heteropraxis of American manifest destiny, then we will need to not just hear and understand but also come alongside and practice with the witness of others, especially those on the margins.
>
> By extension Christian mission in a postcolonial, post-Enlightenment, postmodern, and post-Christendom world can only be redeemed if carried out by eschatological peoples from every tribe, nation, and people who, by being filled with the Spirit of Pentecost, can live in multivocal mutuality and

---

11. Costas, Christ Outside the Gate, 194.

solidarity with one another in anticipation of the reign of God
that is coming and will come.[12]

The church of Jesus Christ in the U.S. will have to evolve out of its
Whiteness and privileged history and become a church that is truly one
body with many members. Different but unified, diverse but beautiful.
This church holds the same people who serve in the CCCU. Therefore, the
CCCU will need to address these issues presented.

RECOMMENDATIONS FOR FUTURE RESEARCH

In every book, the author must choose what will or will not be included.[13]
The same was done here. I could not include many topics that were important, nor could I venture down other pathways that seemed to add value to
this work. I was not able to compare and contrast experiences and issues of
CCCU schools like those that are designated Hispanic Serving Institutions
(HSIs) and examine if diversity issues were different or the same for Latinx
leaders. Would the campus climate or relationships in the leadership be the
same? Would the discrimination and isolation that Latinx leaders experienced be equal to campuses that are not yet designated as HSIs (25 percent
or more of Hispanic student enrollment)?

The CCCU currently has some data on Latinx faculty and people of
color, but this project focused solely on administrators and exclusively used
CRT and LatCrit methods for interviews. Thus, it was important to stay
within the qualitative nature and parameters set out for this research project. However, it would be interesting to discover more about the similarities
or differences between the experiences of Latinx faculty and administrators
in the CCCU. Since faculty have more engagement with students, the perceptions of faculty compared to administrators would have the potential to
shed more light in this area of research.

The five executive Latinx leaders interviewed were mixed in terms of
gender: three were female and two were male. How would this research be
the same or different if the focus was solely on male or female experiences?
Due to the shortage of Latinx leaders these questions had to be bypassed for
now. However, taking these and other additional diversities into account
could make significant contributions for this area of research, and other
research can take on next steps.

---

12. Sechrest et al, Can "White" People Be Saved?, 317.
13. Freeman, Modes of Thinking, 4.

Finally, the three main (or five total) interview questions could be divided, and a single project could elect to focus on one. For instance, one might focus all her energy on the experiences of Latinx leaders, while another might focus on the theological or missiological issues in the CCCU from a Latinx perspective. Lastly, I suppose a whole book could focus on leadership issues that Latinx leaders encounter or experience in Christian higher education. This brings me to my last point: this research was conducted only with Latinx leaders that were currently serving in CCCU schools, but there are more than 900 religiously affiliated institutions of higher education in the U.S.[14] A quantitative or qualitative sampling of these schools would provide a more extensive picture of the situation for Latinx leaders, along with leaders from other underrepresented groups.

LIMITATIONS

This book had several limitations that need to be acknowledged. The first: more interviewees would have been beneficial. For CRT and LatCrit research, an investigator only needs one person to participate, and I had five in the data pool of interviewees, but more participants would have enriched the research. The low participation comes from the fact of the context being examined (the CCCU), and the prerequisite of a Latinx leader having to have served or have been serving in a dean position or higher. This made my potential pool very small. And while others were invited to participate, and I sought out others for the project, due to other professional circumstances they could not participate.

Second, the investigator using qualitative research (CRT) becomes an instrument in methodology. My involvement within the CCCU and other Christian educational institutions and my ascension to the executive level puts me in a unique situation of insider knowledge and personal experiences. In other words, my own familiarity with discrimination and bias in the CCCU and CHE created some sense of predetermined bias as I approached this research and listened to the interviewees tell their stories (in other words, it is difficult to pretend to not know there exists discrimination in an organization when you personally have experienced it). I have with all honesty and integrity tried my best to separate one from the other, but as any researcher should admit, this investigation has been very close to my own personal and professional life. This does not mean that the research here is skewed, but that the reader will need to interpret my findings and recommendations for practice in light of this point.

14. Carpenter et al, Christian Higher Education, 271.

Thirdly, the fact that there are some Christian denominations that still do not ordain women is telling in terms of female leadership at the CEO level in CHE. And while my work did not separate male and female or focus more specifically on issues of gender, identity, or sexual orientation, this intersectionality needs much work. I did try to include this topic in this project; nevertheless, the importance of this subject needs further research and explication.

Lastly, while there are several limitations to this project and I have presented them with all transparency, the hope for the reader (either Latinx or others) is that this new contribution provides a new step in the right direction for a more inclusive experience for all. The Latinx interviewed here, despite being only five, have over 128 years of collective experience in higher education. Therefore, this research project and all that it represents for the CCCU and people of color should not be taken lightly. In fact, the Latinx leaders' experiences provide substantive data supporting the findings that have been presented.

SIGNIFICANCE OF THE STUDY

This book provided a thorough literature review of the experiences of people of color in higher education and Christian higher education (CHE). It also provided a picture of the current landscape of CHE in general as it pertains to Latinx, students, faculty, and staff. Yet, I addressed the lacuna in the CHE research as it pertained to executive Latinx leaders and their experiences, theology and missiology, and leadership theories and practices, and how these factors are incarnate in the CCCU. This was achieved by interviewing five executive Latinx leaders that aligned with the high-prescribed expectations from the researcher.

From the interviews nine themes emerged: (1) systemic racism experienced by Latinx leaders; (2) the notion of Whiteness and mission fit; (3) the glass ceiling; (4) justice and faith; (5) prayer and total dependence on the Holy Spirit; (6) collaborative and community-driven leadership; (7) lifelong learners; (8) chameleon and code-switching leadership; and (9) contextual intelligence and leadership. I then classified these themes under the three main block questions from CRT and LatCrit interviews that described the experiences, theology and missiology, and leadership of the Latinx.

This book provides what other Latinx and people of color aspiring to achieve executive leadership roles in the CCCU can expect from such a journey. Additionally, it clarifies the current landscape for the CCCU as it pertains to the experiences of its leaders from a Latinx perspective. Again, with over 128 years of experience and practice in higher education, these leaders have dedicated their lives to such service and have significant wisdom to impart.

Addressing the experiences, leadership, and theological and missiological frameworks that drive Latinx leaders in CHE is also a contribution to the literature since it adds theory and practice from the margins. This is perhaps the most exciting aspect of this work, since it was provided by using CRT and LatCrit methods (the storytelling and counter-storytelling) of Latinx, rather than their stories being told by the majority culture.

Additionally, the experiences of Latinx leaders in CHE affirm the notion that there exists systemic racism in Christian higher education. Five diverse executive Latinx leaders from five different CCCU schools across the country with over 128 years of experiences across several other institutions of Christian and public higher learning provide a strong argument that addressing diversity issues is the next opportunity for the CCCU if it wants to survive (and thrive!) in the midst of the forecasted demographic shifts and education trends of the twenty-first century.

Finally, I provide recommendations of how the CCCU, Latinx and other leaders of color can address the disparities that continue to endure in the CCCU. These recommendations come from not only the five executive Latinx leaders interviewed in this project, but also my own experiences as a student, administrator and faculty member in the CCCU—which adds up to more than fifteen additional years—totaling 143 years of Latinx experiences within CHE.

CONCLUSION AND PERSONAL REFLECTION

I set-out to research the experiences and expertise of executive Latinx leaders in the CCCU because of my own involvements in Christian higher education (CHE), the limited literature on this topic, and the importance of hearing and learning from these stories. Since I was an executive Latinx leader in the CCCU, I hoped to learn if what I experienced and felt was unique to me, or if similar experiences were shared by others. Lastly, I was driven to discover some type of closure and healing. I am blessed to acknowledge that I have been able to receive both. As a result, my hope is that this book is not seen as something that comes from an angry insider, or a disgruntled ex-partisan, but as a love letter from one who cares deeply about the future of Christian higher education.

Latinx interviewees were very honest and transparent about their experiences in the CCCU. What gives substance to their narratives is their education, years of experience, and sense of calling to CHE. All affirmed they experienced racism, bias, prejudice of some sort, the glass ceiling (for women), discrimination, microaggressions, and the notion of not being mission fit. Likewise, all Latinx leaders felt that their institutions did not take diversity matters seriously enough by lacking accountability, budgets, holistic strategies, and leadership support for the work of diversity, equity, and inclusion. Some of the positive experiences that Latinx leaders described were: a great sense of calling, making a positive difference by transforming people's lives, representing students and the Latinx community, and sharing in God's plan for their schools.

Latinx leaders opened up about their spiritual formation and what theological frameworks guide them to live a life of calling and mission. They reflected on the ways in which their theology changed, developed, or expressed itself in the CCCU. I found that this section of the interviews was the most diverse and unique of all, since Latinx leaders' theology varies considerably. While all described various ways to worship God and find life in prayer and fasting, common ground was discovered in terms of theology and missiology being something that is practiced in community (ortho-praxis) through relationships, and not just doctrine for the sake of doctrine. Said differently, right thinking and right action go hand in hand for these leaders.

All Latinx leaders believed in the power of the Holy Spirit, and that God is still able to change and transform things. All were hopeful and believe the best is yet to come. But most were also concerned for the current state of Christian higher education. The interviewees expressed that one's walk with God was the most important priority; without this, nothing else mattered. One interviewee asserted that you "needed to walk on your knees" when referring to prayer. What has saddened me the most is that only one of five Latinx leaders interviewed, including myself, still serve directly within the CCCU. One more serves at an affiliate school. All others have moved on.[15]

I examined as well the leadership behaviors and traits utilized by Latinx leaders. I wanted to know if there was one specific type of leadership that worked across the CCCU. The tenure and experience of these leaders are essential here, since this experience spoke to the diverse ways in which they served across context and culture. The most valuable insight was the way in which Latinx leaders are able to be "chameleon like" across the CCCU. Although Tomás was the only one who used the word "chameleon," all of

15. My earnest hope is that this project would not only awaken further the CCCU and CHE to the current realities that people of color and Latinx face in their institutions, but that it would serve as enough motivation to seek change for the future survival of CHE.

these leaders emphasized the ability to code-switch, contextualize and be adaptable in their leadership. These are all characteristics of intercultural or contextual leaders. The practices of contextual leadership should be learned and adopted by up-and-coming Latinx leaders, as well as by all CCCU colleagues.

All Latinx leaders understood the complexity of context and how that informed their approach to leading and serving in the CCCU. They were all unwavering about being servants to all, and the importance of being incarnational in relationship-building. Their leadership and theology flourished where social change, justice, and equity are sought after. Overall, these leaders are both competent and contextual in their service to CHE. There is much work to be done and much change that needs to occur for Latinx leaders (and people of color) to truly prosper in this setting.

Lastly, other strategies need to be employed to recruit and retain Latinx leaders. On the subject of academic and leadership searches, Smith states, "leaders should be willing to turn back final candidates if there is no diversity present."[16] Several Latinx leaders experienced first-hand how search committees literally phased out diverse candidates in recruiting and hiring. Smith announces a better strategy for institutions trying to diversify their leadership portfolio:

> If we are to break down the silos of hiring and build the potential for institutional, school, program, and department synergies, leadership has to be engaged early on in the process: the discussion of what is important as revealed in recent program reviews, formulating the job description, creating a competent search committee, selecting a chair, ensuring that the candidate pool is diverse, monitoring that outreach has taken place, supporting efforts to ensure that relevant people have been encouraged to apply, and working to have the department see the institutional and program imperative. As the search proceeds, it is critically important that someone in the administration know what is happening and that necessary supports be in place to facilitate an effective search.[17]

According to the Latinx interviewed, institutions will need to create pipelines, accountability structures, policies and hiring practices, and listen to their community members who will soon reflect the majority-minority student body. This will indeed take some time. Until then, Tomás encourages

16. Smith, Diversity's Promise, 184.
17. Smith, Diversity's Promise, 185.

and recommends that Latinx leaders go back to the hood[18] and eat a good plate of rice, beans and *platanos*. In other words, try to take it easy, do not get anxious, and learn to let go. Sometimes the context is not rewarding and will take more life from you. So, Latinx must stay grounded in their community of faith and find peace in who they are—Latinx.

18. Their neighborhood.

Appendix: Methodology

RESEARCH DESIGN AND METHODOLOGY

This research project is qualitative in nature and utilizes a mixed qualitative method approach in the overall design. As a part of my interdisciplinary and mixed method approach to this research, CRT, LatCrit, intersectionality, and narrative inquiry are employed simultaneously. These approaches all reside within the qualitative research guild and seek to investigate the phenomenological existence of humanity. According to Jeong-Hee Kim, "qualitative research informed by different interpretative paradigms uses words rather than numbers in its analysis and focuses on understanding human action through interpretation rather than prediction and control. It does not reduce research results to certainty and measurable objectivity. Rather, it involves an interpretive, naturalistic approach to research phenomena, making sense of the meaning that people bring to them."[1]

I chose to employ qualitative research because I was studying a complex group of individuals and dealing with a difficult issue within a multifaceted consortium.[2] Therefore, investigating the narratives of the five executive Latinx leaders interviewed was the most important contribution to the data, providing an opportunity to reveal the unknown qualities of the intercultural dynamics between CCCU institutions and this demographic group. It was also important to discover how the participants analyzed and narrated their own reality, which is another significant benefit of employing qualitative methods.

---

1. Kim, *Understanding Narrative Inquiry,* 16.
2. Creswell, *Research Design,* 40.

Qualitative research usually involves studying a human phenomenon that allows the investigator to observe a case and then report on it. As Creswell states:

> Qualitative research begins with assumptions, a worldview, the possible use of a theoretical lens, and the study of research problems inquiring into the meaning individuals or groups ascribe to a social or human problem. To study this problem, qualitative researchers use an emerging qualitative approach to inquiry, the collection of data in a natural setting sensitive to the people and places under study, and data analysis that is inductive and establishes patterns or themes. The final written report or presentation includes the voices of participants, the reflexivity of the researcher, and a complex description and interpretation of the problem, and it extends the literature or signals a call for action.[3]

Out of all the theoretical methodologies that exist, I use CRT and LatCrit the most frequently since they lend themselves naturally to dealing with critical issues of justice, equity, and diversity.

Critical Race Theory (CRT)

My research is situated at the intersection of leadership, intercultural studies, and the Christian higher education (CHE) theoretical field. I use a mixed method approach to investigate the lived experiences of five executive Latinx leaders in the CCCU. I also researched and reviewed the current literature on diversity, equity, and inclusion (DEI) in public higher education in order to inform my Christian context, due to the limited data pertaining to the CCCU. Although there exists considerable literature on Latinx issues (and people of color in general) in higher education literature, the subject of Latinx leadership in the CCCU is at a nascent stage.

I applied storytelling (or counter storytelling) as a component of CRT to address my research problems. Storytelling helps the in-group or majority culture understand the narratives of those who have been marginalized and assigned certain narratives that they themselves may not hold as true.[4] CRT has recognized five basic tenets that provide the framework for this work, specifically challenging societal inequalities that help structures of oppression and privilege for some. These are (a) permanence of race and color-blindness, (b) interest convergence, (c) social construction, (d) differential racialization,

---

3. Creswell, *Research Design*, 37.
4. Delgado and Stefancic, *Critical Race Theory*, 71–72.

and (e) legal or counter-storytelling and narrative analysis.[5] My main focus employing CRT was storytelling, giving voice to the executive Latinx leaders in CHE. As Gloria Ladson-Billings claims, "this scholarly tradition argues against the slow pace of racial reform in the United States. Critical race theory begins with the notion that racism is normal in American society. It departs from mainstream legal scholarship by . . . employing storytelling."[6]

Furthermore, CRT challenges the normalcy of race and ethnic bias in societies and organizations and enables a postmodern and postcolonial world to break with the status quo of the old order. As Delgado and Stefancic declare, "the hope is that well told stories describing the reality of black and brown lives can help readers to bridge the gap between their worlds and those of others."[7] In other words, stories or counter-stories help "shatter complacency and challenge the status quo."[8] CRT challenges the notion that communities of color (specifically Latinx) are a deficit to society and CHE.[9] On the contrary, Latinx hold "cultural wealth" that comes in the value of diverse skillsets, cultural knowledge and responsiveness, code-switching abilities, also bilingual and bicultural, and an array of other assets that often go unacknowledged or recognized by the majority culture.[10]

CRT methodology helps people understand the realities of black and brown people's lived experiences,[11] and these stories allow the "other" to get a glimpse of an unequal world. Additionally, "Storytelling and counter-storytelling these experiences can help strengthen traditions of social, political, and cultural survival and resistance."[12] As Delgado and Stefancic declare, "Critical race theorists have built on everyday experiences with perspective, viewpoint, and the power of stories and persuasion to come to a deeper understanding of how Americans see race."[13] CRT research attempts to expose forms of racism, including "microaggressions, unconscious discrimination, or structural racism" in order to challenge it and build a more just society.[14] Besides opposing all forms of racism and master narratives, CRT also serves

5. Delgado and Stefancic, *Critical Race Theory*, 8–11.

6. Ladson-Billings, "Just What Is Critical Race Theory," 7.

7. Delgado and Stefancic, *Critical Race Theory*, 49.

8. Delgado and Stefancic, *Critical Race Theory*, 72.

9. This is supported by my experience and the experiences of the other Latinx interviewed in this book.

10. Yosso, *Critical Race Counterstories*, 77–79.

11. Solorzano and Yosso, "Critical Race and LatCrit Theory," 32.

12. Solorzano and Yosso, "Critical Race and LatCrit Theory," 32.

13. Delgado and Stefancic, *Critical Race Theory*, 45.

14. Delgado and Stefancic, *Critical Race Theory*, 51.

to eliminate other forms of subordination based on sexual orientation, gender, language and culture, and national origin.[15]

Lastly, there are three forms of storytelling in CRT, according to Daniel Solorzano and Tara Yosso: Personal stories or narratives that are (1) autobiographical in nature telling the person's experience with sexism or racism; (2) Other people's stories or narratives—usually biographical in nature and voice the experiences of a person of color in U.S. institutions and their sociohistorical contexts; and, (3) Composite stories or narratives—utilizing both autobiography and biography along with other data points with composite characters and situating them within a specific context.[16]

Latina/o Critical Race Theory (LatCrit)

Latina/o Critical Race Theory (LatCrit) is also used in this research since the participants interviewed are Latinx. LatCrit, like CRT, gives voice to the Latinx leaders in similar ways, but focuses mainly on the intersections of identity and helps to analyze issues that CRT cannot or does not, "like language, immigration, ethnicity, culture, identity, phenotype, and sexuality."[17] While issues of race and racialization are key components that CRT addresses, LatCrit interrogates how race affects the Latinx population in society. For example, Lopez and Haney declared, "the language of race will be indispensable to LatCrit Theory, affording not only a manner of focusing on the experiences and conditions of our communities but a basis for responding to the iniquities of racialization."[18]

LatCrit incorporates the following four functions, according to Francisco Valdes: (a) the production of knowledge, (b) the advancement of transformation, (c) the expansion and connection of struggle(s), and (d) the cultivation of community and coalition.[19] These functions, along with CRT, give the Latinx leaders in this project a counter voice to the master narratives. LatCrit offers "epistemological, methodological, and theoretical contributions to educational research" through the *testimonios* of the Latinx leaders.[20] Lastly, LatCrit addresses the unique contextual social, political, and systemic racist realities that Latinx face on a daily basis. As Solorzano and Yosso state, "we believe a strength of critical race and LatCrit theory and

15. Solorzano and Yosso, "Critical Race and LatCrit Theory," 25.
16. Solorzano and Yosso, "Critical Race and LatCrit Theory, 32–34.
17. Villalpando, "Practical Considerations," 43.
18. Haney-Lopez, "Race, Ethnicity, Erasure," 69.
19. Valdes, "Foreword: Under Construction," 78.
20. Fernandez, "Telling Stories about School," 47–48.

methodology is the validation and combination of the theoretical, empirical, and experiential knowledge. Through our counter-narrative, we delve into the lives of human characters who experience daily the intersections of racism, sexism, and classism."[21] Therefore, using LatCrit Theory will allow for the Latinx experience to speak for itself through counter-narratives.

A Christian Rationale for Using CRT

As previously mentioned, Critical Race Theory (CRT) comes out of the legal field of scholarship and practice. It started as a movement to address the lack of progress dealing with racism in the U.S., post-Civil Rights Era. As Delgado and Stefancic declare:

> Critical Race Theory sprang up in the 1970's, as a number of lawyers, activists, and legal scholars across the country realized, more or less simultaneously, that the heady advances of civil rights era of the 1960's had stalled and, in many respects, were being rolled back. Realizing that new theories and strategies were needed to combat the subtler forms of racism that were gaining ground, early writers, such as Derrick Bell, Alan Freeman, and Richard Delgado, put their minds to the task.[22]

At this point it is important to mention that CRT was birthed from a place seeking justice and equity, and as a movement to speak to the social inequities that people of color were facing in the U.S., including inadequate employment and wages, lack of educational opportunities, and injustice in the criminal justice system. Nevertheless, there has been some critic from Christian evangelical circles about CRT, which can be summarized as follows: (1) CRT participates in a liberal agenda, emphasizing social justice issues, which is contradictory to the central role of the church;[23] (2) CRT essentially perpetuates reverse racism by not allowing White people to challenge the stories of people of color;[24] and lastly, (3) it divides people more, rather than participating in the work of unification, since it focuses heavily on race and ethnicity and not the neutrality of the Kingdom of God in terms of identity.[25]

21. Solorzano and Yosso, "Critical Race and LatCrit Theory," 489.

22. Delgado and Stefancic, *Critical Race Theory*, 4.

23. Diaz, "Is Critical Race Theory Anti-Christian?"

24. Shenvi, "Critical Race Theory and Christianity."

25. Pulpit & Pen, "4 Main Things." I have only identified these three issues as a conversational starter and because of their significance and relevance to this research project. However, conducting a Google search with the question "Is Critical Race Theory

I believe it is essential to provide some rationale regarding why it is acceptable for Christians to use CRT as a methodology to address disparities within Christian communities dealing with people of color. The Bible speaks frequently about the Law, and the importance of citizens abiding by legal codes. In fact, the Lord gave Israel a set of Laws known as the Ten Commandments (see Exod 20:117; Deut 5:621) in order to prosper them (Deut 29:9), serve as a guide until Christ (Gal 3:24), and thereafter to provide the standard of living for the disciples of Jesus (John 8:31). In simplest terms, the Scriptures, consisting of the Old (OT) and the New Testament (NT) serve as covenants between the people and God. This word is what the Psalmist said would be a lamp to his feet and light to his path (Ps 119:105). In other words, the written covenant provides the direction that people need in order to live according to the Scriptures.

The Law and Scriptures in the OT and in the NT are justice driven. A short reading of the prophets brings light and speaks against the oppression of the people. And even Jesus asserts as a new commandant (John 13:34–35) that people should love each other and God. As an example, refer to the following Scriptures:

- "Defend the weak and the fatherless; uphold the cause of the poor and the oppressed." (Ps 82:3, NIV)

- "Learn to do right; seek justice. Defend the oppressed. Take up the cause of the fatherless; plead the case of the widow." (Isa 1:17, NIV)

- "He has shown you, O mortal, what is good. And what does the Lord require of you? To act justly and to love mercy and to walk humbly with your God." (Mic 6:8, NIV)

- "Woe to you, Pharisees, because you give God a tenth of your mint, rue and all other kinds of garden herbs, but you neglect justice and the love of God. You should have practiced the latter without leaving the former undone." (Luke 11:42, NIV)

- "Teacher, which is the greatest commandment in the Law?" Jesus replied: "'Love the Lord your God with all your heart and with all your soul and with all your mind.' This is the first and greatest commandment. And the second is like it: 'Love your neighbor as yourself.' All the Law and the Prophets hang on these two commandments." (Matt 22:36–40, NIV)

If we apply the Scriptures along with the principles of CRT as our hermeneutic, we discover a method that is helpful in the holy work of addressing

---

Christian?" produces 87,000,000 results. This is another book in itself.

issues of oppression, discrimination, and racism. Some of the above-named issues with CRT are even clarified by the Scriptures themselves. Justice is, in fact, a gospel agenda, as showcased by the Scriptures above. Even throughout the Scriptures, differences among people are presented concerning race, ethnicity, and gender (see Rev 7; Acts 2, and Gen 1:27). In other words, the Bible doesn't ascribe to colorblindness as a way forward for the Christian community. Furthermore, the early accounts of the gospel were transferred through oral traditions in the primitive church, and today we uphold this tradition by giving testimonies in church services.

CRT, therefore, is a methodology that aligns well with Christianity as a justice and equity-driven movement seeking to liberate the oppressed and to bring justice to the marginalized, laboring under systems of domination and racism. While CRT does provide the avenue for people of color the opportunity to speak out their stories, like Christians testifying in church services, there is, in fact, room for challenging these stories. Our common Christian identity allows us to walk together and listen to one another with love and respect.[26]

Intersectionality

Another important method I engage in this research project is intersectionality, which is used as an analytical tool to gain deeper understanding of the complexities around the world, as a form of critical inquiry and praxis, and to create a just future within human contexts. Collins and Bilge offer the following as a description of intersectionality:

> Intersectionality is a way of understanding and analyzing the complexity in the world, in people, and in human experiences. The events and conditions of social and political life and the self can seldom be understood and as shaped by one factor. They are generally shaped by many factors in diverse and mutually influencing ways. When it comes to social inequality, people's lives and the organization of power in a given society are better understood as being shaped not by a single axis of social division, be it race or gender or class, but by many axes that work together and influence each other. Intersectionality as an

---

26. A greater demonstration of the use of CRT and LatCrit is found in the testimonies in the book, while the need and rationale for the use of these approaches in terms of how groups have historically been marginalized and why they need their own voice is found in Chapter 3.

analytic tool gives people better access to the complexity of the world and of themselves.[27]

The term *intersectionality* was first developed by Kimberle Crenshaw to cast light on the neglect that women of color were experiencing in positionality and experience, in terms of racism and sexism. Crenshaw argued:

> that Black women are sometimes excluded from feminist theory and antiracist policy discourse because both are predicated on a discrete set of experiences that often does not accurately reflect the interaction of race and gender. These problems of exclusion cannot be solved simply by including Black women within an already established analytical structure. Because the intersectional experience is greater than the sum of racism and sexism, any analysis that does not take intersectionality into account cannot sufficiently address the particular manner in which Black women are subordinated.[28]

My use of intersectionality and CRT is to discover the intersections of identity and life experiences of Latinx leaders and their stories in Christian higher education (CHE). CHE has often addressed diversity issues from one perspective or axis, at times leaving out aspects of life, experience and work that matter the most. This method gives the researcher another lens for which to investigate narratives from five diverse participants and their experiences, missiology and theology, and leadership within the CCCU. Since all differences among people and their organizations matter, intersectionality offers language for those involved.

Intersectionality also examines as an analytical tool how "power relations are intertwined and mutually constructing. Race, class, gender, sexuality, dis/ability, ethnicity, nation, religion, and age are categories of analysis, terms that reference important social divisions. But they are also categories that gain meaning from power relations of racism, sexism, heterosexism, and class exploitation."[29] I use intersectionality as a method to examine the ways in which "inequality, relationality, power, social context, complexity, and social justice" operate within the CCCU and the relational experiences of executive Latinx leaders.

The use of intersectionality as a theoretical framework allows me to probe the multiple modes of oppressive social and political structures towards Latinx. According to Banda, "Structural inequality and oppression

---

27. Collins and Bilge, *Intersectionality*, 193.

28. Crenshaw, "Demarginalizing the Intersection," 140.

29. Collins and Bilge, *Intersectionality*, 7.

often intersect at multiple dimensions such as, to name a few, race, ethnicity, gender, socioeconomic status, and sexual orientation, respectively."[30] Therefore, utilizing intersectionality is not accepting of the status quo, but challenges structures of oppression and discrimination, and is critical of anything that stands in the way of justice for human thriving.[31] Therefore, this method is used in order to discover and present the intersections of identity of the participants and how we can make sense of current realities in the CCCU.

Narrative Inquiry

Narrative inquiry is about "knowing and telling."[32] Kim states, "narrative is one of the few human endeavors that is widely spread as a basic aspect of human life and an essential strategy of human expression."[33] Narratives put together are what make up a story. Therefore, the narratives that are gathered of the five executive Latinx leaders are woven together to tell the stories of their experience in CHE. In other words, narrative inquiry is about systematizing human experience.[34]

For narrative research, the experience of those telling their stories is most valuable. Souto-Manning claims: "Narratives are how we make sense of what we know, what we feel and experience in the world in which we live. Personal identities are constructed and (re)conceptualized as we share our narratives."[35] Narrative is concerned with how people view or experience the world in which they live.[36] Connelly and Clandinin state:

> Viewed this way, narrative is the phenomenon studied in inquiry. Narrative inquiry, the study of experience as story, then, is first and foremost a way of thinking about experience. Narrative inquiry as a methodology entails a view of the phenomenon. To use narrative inquiry methodology is to adopt a particular narrative view of experience as phenomena under study.[37]

30. Banda, "Inside Looking Out," 2.
31. Collins and Bilge, *Intersectionality*, 30.
32. Kim, *Understanding Narrative Inquiry*, 6.
33. Kim, *Understanding Narrative Inquiry*, 6.
34. Souto-Manning, "Critical Narrative Analysis," 162.
35. Souto-Manning, "Critical Narrative Analysis," 162.
36. Kim, *Understanding Narrative Inquiry*, 18.
37. As quoted in Kim, *Understanding Narrative Inquiry*, 6.

Using this narrative inquiry approach side-by-side with counter storytelling from CRT allowed the voices, experiences, and competencies of the Latinx leaders from the CCCU to be heard from a place of neutrality.

RESEARCH DESIGN

This book utilizes a mixed methods approach via various qualitative strategies to find meaning of the narratives of five executive Latinx leaders in Christian higher education (CHE). To obtain meaningful data from these leaders, it was important to ask questions in these three main areas: (1) what are your overall lived experiences in the Council of Christian Colleges and Universities (CCCU)? (2) what theological or missiological frameworks drive you or enable you to serve in the CCCU? and, (3) what are the main leadership approaches needed by Latinx in order to navigate the CCCU successfully? Two years after asking the participants these questions, I circled back and asked two more questions: (1) is there anything else that you would like to add? and, (2) is there anything from current events that you think or feel that applies to diversity, equity, and inclusion (DEI) in CHE?

These interview questions through CRT gave me the opportunity to understand at a deeper level the complexities power, privilege, and systemic critical issues within the CCCU and Latinx communities. Learning of the missiological and theological frameworks provided clarity on why and how some things are carried out in the CCCU, since they are mostly confessional schools. And finally, inquiring about the Latinx leadership was a complete joy since it afforded the occasion to shed light on what other up-and-coming Latinx leaders need to learn in order to navigate the complexities of predominantly White institutions. The official questions follow.

Interview Questions

Some of the interview questions are adopted or modified from Michael Moffit's dissertation, *A Narrative Study of the Experiences of Executive Administrators of Color Who Work at Religiously-Affiliated Higher Education Institutions.*[38] His questions were addressed to a small group of people of color in religiously affiliated institutions. My questions are strictly for Latinx serving in CCCU schools.

1. What are the experiences of Executive Latinx Administrators at CCCU schools?

38. Moffit, *Narrative Study,* 147.

- What encumbers Latinx leaders to progress in Christian higher education?

- What barriers in the workplace have you encountered while advancing in your career in Christian higher education? (sexism, racism, discrimination and so forth)

- What are contextual barriers you may encounter that hinder you from advancement to the executive level of higher education? (Social, internal, institutional/organizational)

2. What theological and missiological frameworks drive Latinx leaders in Christian higher education?

- How has your theology, missiology, and faith changed or strengthened since serving in Christian higher education?

- What type of spiritual formation is needed to be an executive leader in Christian higher education?

- What do you feel or think (or perceive) from your White or other colleagues in Christian higher education about your views theologically?

- What is your observation of being "mission fit" or not?

- Is there anything I am not asking that has impacted you theologically in Christian higher education?

3. What type of intercultural, multicultural, and or contextual leadership is needed by Latinx leaders to succeed in Christian higher education?

- What is your preferred leadership style, approach, theory, or posture within the CCCU?

- Tell me how you decided to pursue an executive leadership position within the CCCU.

- Describe how you prepared and made yourself eligible for this type of a position.

- What was your first impression as an administrator of color working in a monocultural environment?

- As one who has experience working within religiously-affiliated institutions, what are the observed social realities of working within a mostly homogeneous environment?

- Talk about your experience at a Predominantly White Institution while serving as an administrator of color within the CCCU.

- What coping mechanisms and strategies have you used in your career?

- What are the top three pieces of advice you want to give up-and-coming Latinx leaders in Christian higher education?

Additional questions added two years later:

4. Is there anything else that you may want to add to this project that you may have left out previously?

5. Is there anything from current events that you think or feel applies to diversity, equity, and inclusion in Christian higher education?

It was important to ask questions that could help me understand the diversity of experiences lived by these leaders, but also to determine if there were similarities, differences, or contradictions, not only related to my own experiences within the CCCU, but to those of the other Latinx leaders in CHE. Freeman states:

> All social scientific research involves a taking stock of what is being worked with and a process for making a statement about the topic of inquiry. In other words, all research involves some sort of data identification, organization, selection, creation, recognition, and some sort of transformation of what is identified, organized, selected, created, recognized into a statement about the topic of inquiry or "findings."[39]

These interview questions helped me to organize and analyze the data being collected and interpreted. The data was sorted into themes as they surfaced from Latinx interviews and categorized according to the diversity literature.

Participants, Recruitment, and Ethical Standards

The executive Latinx leaders selected to participate in this project all hold (or held) a position of dean or above at the time of interview (that is, vice president, provost, etc.) and are serving (or have served) in a member or affiliate member school of the CCCU. All participants hold a PhD degree, are from Latinx family origin, some held faculty roles before becoming administrators, and some still teach. All their names are concealed for identity

---

39. Freeman, *Modes of Thinking*, 3.

purposes due to the limited handful to choose from in the CCCU. Three are female and two are male, and the names given to them are: Marisol, Ruth, Yanisa, Tomás and Josue.[40]

I was able to recruit participants by the leading of mutual colleagues and exposure to them in the CCCU diversity conference in 2015–2016 in Chicago. Due to the limited pool who had served as a dean or greater, the choices were simple. Because the CCCU is a consortium of over 140 institutions, these participants were chosen to describe their lived experiences and to reflect on the commonalities of the expressed phenomena.

Participants were originally asked by text message if they had interest in participating in such a research project. After they agreed, an email of invitation was sent, along with two documents: (1) the consent document, which they all needed to sign and return by email, and (2) the Human Subjects Review document that was approved by Fuller Theological Seminary for their review and participation by interview. Once all the paperwork was collected electronically, the first round of sixty-to-ninety-minute interviews was scheduled by email to be conducted through Adobe Connect or Skype. The audio portion of interviews was recorded by smartphone for accuracy (but not the video component) and transferred to my MacBook Air. Notes were concurrently taken to complement the recording. Interviews were transcribed using Speech Tools in Microsoft Word. Transcriptions, video recordings and notes were used for the upmost accuracy for quotes and data analysis.

Delimitations

1. This research project focuses solely on educational institutions that belong to the Council of Christian Colleges and Universities.

2. Although there exist Latinx in different types of leadership within these universities and colleges, I only research, study, and or investigate those who hold positions of dean and above (that is, vice president, provost, president, chief academic officers).

3. The Latinx leaders interviewed served at least three years, but some more than 20, in executive roles, providing validity of data to be built upon for future research.

---

40. All interviews are confidential, and the names of interviewees are withheld by mutual agreement.

4. There exists a need for much research in DEI issues for CHE, but this project exclusively focused on Latinx executive leadership.

5. There were three women and two men as participants. A stronger study would focus mainly on one variable or the other (for example, five Latinx woman or five Latinx men.)

Definitions

The following definitions provide framing for the book.

1. Christian higher education (CHE)—A college or university that has Christian religious affiliation (such as those that belong to the CCCU).

2. Council of Christian Colleges and Universities—The Council for Christian Colleges & Universities (CCCU) is a higher education association of 180 Christian institutions around the world. The 140 member campuses in North America are all regionally accredited, comprehensive colleges and universities with curricula rooted in the arts and sciences. In addition, sixty-five affiliate campuses from twenty countries are part of the CCCU. The CCCU encompasses thirty-five Protestant denominations as well as Roman Catholic institutions in its membership. The CCCU is a tax-exempt 501(c)(3) nonprofit organization headquartered in the historic Capitol Hill district of Washington, D.C.[1]

3. Latino and Latina (Hispanic, Latino/a or Latina/o)—are "terms that define the unity of various U.S. communities that have ties to Latin America or with the Spanish-speaking world."[2]

4. Latinx—According to Cristobal Salinas and Adele Lozano, Latinx is a gender-neutral term that began to be utilized in 2014, supplementing the traditional words of Hispanic or Latino.[3] All terms are used interchangeably in this project for the same group of people.

5. Leadership—is the "process whereby an individual influences a group of individuals to achieve a common goal."[4]

---

1. Council for Christian Colleges and Universities.
2. Martínez, *Walk with the People*, 16.
3. Salinas and Lozano, "Mapping and Recontextualizing," 17.
4. Northouse, *Leadership: Theory and Practice*, 6.

6. White privilege—"much of U.S. history embeds privilege for Whites in general, and White upper-class men in particular, in voting, landowning, and access to higher education. While this privilege is no longer explicit, as it often was in earlier eras, there is a growing body of literature documenting that the pattern continues, though in subtler and less visible ways."[5]

7. People of color—anyone who is not White or Euro-American.

8. Diversity—Issues dealing with race, nationality, culture, access and inclusion, equity for all, ethnicity, gender, religion, veteran, disability and ability status, and sexual orientation. Please note, there are many definitions of diversity, but I will apply this to the context of Christian higher education and focus particularly on race and ethnicity.

9. Critical Race Theory (CRT)—CRT is a "collection of activists and scholars interested in studying and transforming the relationship between race, racism, and power. The movement considers many of the same issues that conventional civil rights and ethnic studies discourses take up, but places these issues in a broader perspective that includes economics, history, context, group-and self-interest, and even feelings and the unconscious. Unlike traditional civil rights, which stresses incrementalism and step-by-step progress, critical race theory questions the very foundations of the liberal order, including equality theory, legal reasoning, Enlightenment rationalism, and neutral principles of constitutional law."[6]

10. Latino/a Critical Race Theory (LatCrit Theory)—is a tenet from CRT that has its particulars in dealing with the Latinx community, stressing societal and identity intersections.

5. Smith, *Diversity's Promise*, 10.

6. Delgado and Stefancic, *Critical Race Theory*, 3.

About the Author

PETER RIOS, DSL, PHD, is a Lecturer at Penn State and the Founder of Peter Rios Consulting. He has served diverse organizations including businesses, religious institutions, government, higher education and non-profits in the areas of diversity, equity and inclusion; leadership development and change.

His extensive professional and academic experience has made him a sought-out keynote and conference speaker. Rios has been invited to speak and train leaders, nationally and internationally. He is also a veteran of the United States Marine Corps.

Peter has served as an adjunct professor at several institutions teaching undergraduate and graduate students in organizational leadership, business management, religious and cultural studies. Rios has also been a vice president at two universities. Prior to academia, Peter was involved in pastoral ministry for over ten years and has over twenty years of leadership development experience.

Rios holds a PhD in Intercultural Studies from Fuller Graduate Schools, a Doctorate in Strategic Leadership (DSL) from Regent University, completed doctoral work at the University of Southern California, and an MA from Northeastern Seminary. He is married to Dr. Ruby Gonzalez-Rios, a cancer and infectious disease researcher. For more information, please visit peterriosconsulting.com.

Bibliography

Banda, Rosa M. "From the Inside Looking Out: Latinas Intersectionality and Their Engineering Departments." *International Journal of Qualitative Studies in Education* 33:3 (2020) 116.

Barna, George. *The Power of Vision: Discover and Apply God's Plan for your Life and Ministry*. Ventura, CA: Regal, 2009.

Barna Group. *Hispanic America; Faith, Values, and Priorities*. Ventura, CA: Barna Group, 2012.

Bastedo, Michael N., et al. *American Higher Education in the Twenty First Century: Social, Political, and Economic Challenges*. 4th ed. Baltimore: Johns Hopkins University Press, 2016.

Batista, Angela E. et al, eds. *Latinx/a/os in Higher Education: Exploring Identity, Pathways, and Success*. 1st ed. Washington, DC: NASPA-Student Affairs Administrators in Higher Education, 2018.

Bevans, Stephen B. *Models of Contextual Theology*. Faith and Culture Series, Maryknoll, NY: Orbis, 1992.

Bolman, Lee G., and Terrence E Deal. *Reframing Organizations: Artistry, Choice, and Leadership*. 5th ed. San Francisco: Jossey-Bass, 2013.

Bordas, Juana. *Salsa, Soul, and Spirit: Leadership for a Multicultural Age*. 2nd ed. San Francisco: Berrett-Koehler, 2012.

———. *The Power of Latino Leadership Culture, Inclusion, and Contribution*. 1st ed. San Francisco: Berrett-Koehler, 2013.

Boschma, Jamie. "Fourteen States Have Enacted 22 New Laws Making It Harder to Vote." https://www.cnn.com/2021/05/28/politics/voter-suppression-restrictive-voting -bills/index.html.

Bradley, B. Anthony, ed. *Aliens in the Promised Land: Why Minority Leadership is Overlooked in White Christian Churches and Institutions*. Phillipsburg, NJ: Zondervan, 2013.

Branson, Mark Lau, and Juan Francisco Martínez. *Churches, Cultures, and Leadership: A Practical Theology of Congregations and Ethnicities*. Downers Grove, IL: InterVarsity Academic, 2011.

Brooks, Stephen, et al. *Understanding American Politics*. 2nd ed. University of Toronto Press, 2013.

Brown, S. E., Santiago, D., and Adam, M. (2005, Jan 31). "¡Excelencia In Education, Inc! Leaders Address Role of Hispanic-serving Institutions." *The Hispanic Outlook in Higher Education* 15:17 Accessed on April 25, 2017, http://0-search.proquest.com. library.regent.edu/docview/219321634?accountid=13479.

Butler, Anthea D. *White Evangelical Racism: The Politics of Morality in America*. Chapel Hill, NC: University of North Carolina Press, 2021.

Carpenter, Joel, et al, eds. *Christian Higher Education: A Global Reconnaissance*. Grand Rapids, MI: Wm B. Eerdmans, 2014.

Carter, J. Kameron. *Race: A Theological Account*. Oxford: Oxford University Press, 2008.

Chen, Guo-Ming and William J. Starosta. *Foundations of Intercultural Communication*. 2nd ed. Lanham, MD: University Press of America, 2005.

Chun, Edna, and Alvin Evans. *Leading a Diversity Culture Shift in Higher Education: Comprehensive Organizational Learning Strategies*. New York: Routledge, 2018.

Cleveland, Christena. *Disunity in Christ: Uncovering the Hidden Forces That Keep Us Apart*. Downers Grove, IL: InterVarsity, 2013.

Clinton, J. Robert. *The Making of a Leader: Recognizing the Lessons and Stages of Leadership Development*. Colorado Springs, CO: NavPress, 2012.

Collins, Christopher S., and Alexander Jun. *White Out: Understanding White Privilege and Dominance in the Modern Age*. New York: Peter Lang, 2017.

Collins, Patricia Hill and Sirma Bilge. *Intersectionality*. Cambridge: Polity, 2016.

Cone, James H. *The Cross and the Lynching Tree*. Maryknoll, NY: Orbis, 2011.

Conrad, Clifton, and Marybeth Gasman. *Educating a Diverse Nation: Lessons from Minority-Serving Institutions*. Cambridge: Harvard University Press, 2015.

Cooper, Diane, et al, eds. *Multiculturalism on Campus*. Sterling, VA: Stylus, 2011.

Cornell, Stephen E., and Douglas Hartmann. *Ethnicity and Race: Making Identities in a Changing World*. 2nd ed. Thousand Oaks, CA: Pine Forge, an Imprint of SAGE, 2007.

Costas, Orlando E. *Christ Outside the Gate: Mission Beyond Christendom*. Maryknoll, NY: Orbis, 1982.

Council for Christian Colleges and Universities. "About Our Work and Mission." https://www.cccu.org/about/#heading-our-work-and-mission-0.

———. "The Case for Christian Higher Education." Washington, D.C.: Council of Christian Colleges and Universities, 2018. https://www.cccu.org/wp-content/uploads/2018/08/2018-Case-for-CHE_WEB_pages.pdf.

———. 2020. *Advance Magazine. Diversity Matters: Race, Ethnicity, and Christian Higher Education*. Washington, D.C.: Council of Christian Colleges and Universities, Spring 2020. https://www.cccu.org/wp-content/uploads/2020/04/Spring-2020-Advance-low-res.pdf.

Crenshaw, Kimberle. "Demarginalizing the Intersection of Race and Sex: A Black Feminist Critique of Antidiscrimination Doctrine, Feminist Theory, and Antiracist Politics." *University of Chicago Legal Forum* 1989:1:8 (1989) 139–167.

Creswell, John W. *Research Design: Qualitative, Quantitative, and Mixed Methods Approaches*. 4th ed. Thousand Oaks, CA: SAGE, 2014.

Davis, M. A. 1997. "Latino Leadership Development: Beginning on Campus." *National Civic Review* 86:3 (1997) 227–233.

De Jong, Rob-Jan. *Anticipate: The Art of Leading by Looking Ahead*. New York: American Management Association, 2015.

De La Torre, Miguel A. *Burying White Privilege: Resurrecting a Badass Christianity*. Grand Rapids, MI: Wm. B. Eerdmans, 2019.

———. *Decolonizing Christianity: Becoming Badass Believers*. Grand Rapids, MI: Wm. B. Eerdmans, 2021.

———. *The Politics of Jesus: A Hispanic Political Theology*. Religion in the Modern World. Lanham: Rowman & Littlefield, 2015.

———. *Reading the Bible from the Margins*. Maryknoll, NY: Orbis, 2002.

Delgado, Richard and Jean Stefancic. *Critical Race Theory: An Introduction*. 2nd ed. New York: New York University Press, 2012.

———. *Critical Race Theory: The Cutting Edge*. 3rd ed. Philadelphia: Temple University Press, 2013.

DeNavas-Walt, Carmen and Bernadette D. Proctor. 2014. "Income and Poverty in the United States: 2014." Washington, D.C.: United States Census Bureau, 2014.

DePouw, Christin. "Intersectionality and Critical Race Parenting." *International Journal of Qualitative Studies in Education* 31:1 (2018) 55–69.

Diaz III, Hiram R. "Is Critical Race Theory Anti-Christian? Yes." *Biblical Trinitarian: Apologetics in the Sight of God*. November 7, 2018. http://www.biblicaltrinitarian. com/2018/11/is-critical-race-theory-anti-christian.html.

Diaz-Isasi, Ada Maria, and Fernando F. Segovia, eds. *Hispanic/Latino Theology: Challenge and Promise*. Minneapolis, MN: Augsburg Fortress, 1996.

Djupe, Paul A., and Ryan L. Claassen. *The Evangelical Crackup? The Future of the Evangelical-Republican Coalition*. Religious Engagement in Democratic Politics. Philadelphia, PA: Temple University Press, 2018.

Dutton, Jack. "Critical Race Theory Is Banned in These States." https://www.newsweek. com/critical-race-theory-banned-these-states-1599712.

Emerson, M. O., and C. Smith. *Divided by Faith: Evangelical Religion and the Problem of Race in America*. Oxford: Oxford University Press, 2000.

Escobar, Samuel. *The New Global Mission: The Gospel from Everywhere to Everyone*. Christian Doctrine in Global Perspective. Downers Grove, IL: InterVarsity, 2003.

Fernandez, L. "Telling Stories About School: Using Critical Race and Latino Critical Theories to Document Latina/Latino Education and Resistance." *Qualitative Inquiry* 8 (2002) 45–65.

Freeman, Melissa. *Modes of Thinking for Qualitative Data Analysis*. New York: Routledge, 2017.

Fubara, E. I., et al. "Applying Diversity Management Principles to Institutions of Christian Higher Education." *Christian Higher Education* 10:2 (2011) 112–131.

Gibbs, Eddie. *Leadership Next: Changing Leaders in a Changing Culture*. Downers Grove, IL: InterVarsity 2005.

Glanzer, Perry L, et al. *Restoring the Soul of the University: Unifying Christian Higher Education in a Fragmented Age*. Downers Grove, IL: InterVarsity, 2017.

Gómez de Torres, A.M. "Latina Leaders in Higher Education: Understanding their Paths to Leadership." PhD diss., University of La Verne, 2013. http://libproxy.usc. edu/login?url=https://search-proquest-com.libproxy1.usc.edu/docview/1467750 664?accountid=14749.

Gordon, Adam. *Future Savvy: Identifying Trends to Make Better Decisions, Manage Uncertainty, and Profit from Change*. New York: American Management Association, 2009.

Greenleaf, Robert K. *The Servant as Leader*. Westfield, IN: The Greenleaf Center for Servant Leadership, 2008.

Haney-Lopez, Ian F. "Race, Ethnicity, Erasure: The Salience of Race to LatCrit Theory." *California Law Review* 85, 5 (1997) 57.

Hanshaw, Mark and Timothy Moore, eds. *Intersections: Faith, Church, and the Academy.* Nashville, TN: General Board of Higher Education & Ministry, 2018.

Harvey, Jennifer. *Dear White Christians: For Those Still Longing for Racial Reconciliation.* Prophetic Christianity. Grand Rapids, MI: Wm. B. Eerdmans, 2014.

Hays, J. Daniel. *From Every People and Nation: A Biblical Theology of Race.* New Studies in Biblical Theology 14. Leicester, UK: Apollos, 2013.

Heibert, Paul G. *The Gospel in Human Contexts: Anthropological Explorations for Contemporary Missions.* Grand Rapids, MI: Baker Academic, 2009.

Henck, Anita Fitzgerald. (2011). "Walking the Tightrope: Christian Colleges and Universities in a Time of Change." *Christian Higher Education* 10:34 (2011) 196214.

Hill, Daniel. *White Awake: An Honest Look at What It Means to Be White.* Downers Grove, IL: InterVarsity, 2017.

Hispanic Association of Colleges and Universities. 2018. "Fact Sheet Hispanic Higher Education and HISs." Hispanic Association of Colleges and Universities, 2018. https://www.hacu.net/hacu/HSI_Fact_Sheet.asp.

Hopkins, Dwight N. *Being Human: Race, Culture, and Religion.* Minneapolis, MN: Fortress, 2015.

Hughes, L. Richard, and Katherine Colarelli Beatty. *Becoming a Strategic Leader: Your Role in your Organization's Enduring Success.* San Francisco, CA: Jossey Bass, 2005.

Hughes, L. Richard, et al. *Leadership: Enhancing the Lessons of Experience.* 8th ed. New York: McGraw-Hill, 2015.

Isazi-Diaz, Ada Maria and Fernando F. Segovia, eds. *Hispanic Latino Theology: Challenge and Promise.* Philadelphia: Fortress, 1996.

Jennings, Willie James. *The Christian Imagination: Theology and the Origins of Race.* New Haven, CT: Yale University Press, 2010.

Jones, P. Robert. *The End of White Christian America.* New York: Simon and Schuster, 2016.

———. 2020. *White Too Long: The Legacy of White Supremacy in American Christianity.* New York, NY: Simon & Schuster, 2020.

Joshi, Khyati Y. *White Christian Privilege: The Illusion of Religious Equality in America.* New York: New York University Press, 2020.

Jun, Alexander, et al. *White Jesus: The Architecture of Racism in Religion and Education.* 1st ed. New York: Peter Lang, 2018.

Kemeny, P.C. *Faith, Freedom, and Higher Education: Historical Analysis and Contemporary Reflections.* Eugene, OR: Pickwick, 2013.

Kim, Jeong-Hee. *Understanding Narrative Inquiry: The Crafting and Analysis of Stories as Research.* Thousand Oaks, CA, 2015.

Klenke, K. *Women in Leadership: Contextual Dynamics and Boundaries.* Bingley, UK: Emerald, 2011.

Kouzes, James, and Barry Posner. *The Leadership Challenge: How to Make Extraordinary Things Happen in Organizations.* 5th ed. San Francisco, CA: Jossey-Bass, 2012.

Krogstad, Jens Manuel. "5 Facts about Latinos and Education." *Pew Research Center,* 2016. http://www.pewresearch.org/fact-tank/2016/07/28/5-facts-about-latinos-and-education/.

Kruse, Kevin Michael. *One Nation Under God: How Corporate America Invented Christian America.* New York: Basic Books, 2015.

Kutz, Matthew. *Contextual Intelligence: How Thinking in 3D Can Help Resolve Complexity, Uncertainty, and Ambiguity.* Cham, Switzerland: Springer International, 2017.

Ladson-Billings, Gloria. "Just what is Critical Race Theory and What's it Doing in a Nice Field like Education?" *International Journal of Qualitative Studies in Education* 11:1 (1998) 724.

Lang, Justin A., and Lonnie Yandell. "Diversity Language as System Maintenance: Toward Alternative Frameworks for Addressing Racism at Predominantly White Institutions." *Christian Higher Education* 18:5 (2019) 343–55.

Lara-Braud, Jorge. "Hispanic-American Spirituality: A Reformed Theological Reflection." *Church & Society* 90:3 (2000) 88–103.

Leedy, Paul D, and Jeanne Ellis Ormrod. *Practical Research: Planning and Design.* 10th ed. Boston: Pearson, 2013.

León David J, and Ruben Orlando Martinez, eds. *Latino College Presidents: In Their Own Words.* Diversity in Higher Education 13. Bingley, UK: Emerald, 2013.

Lewis, Verlan. *Ideas of Power: The Politics of American Party Ideology Development.* Cambridge: Cambridge University Press, 2019.

Lingenfelter, Judith E. and Sherwood G. Lingenfelter. *Teaching Cross-Culturally: An Incarnational Model for Learning and Teaching.* Grand Rapids, MI: Baker Academic, 2003.

Lingenfelter, Sherwood G. *Leading Cross-Culturally: Covenant Relationships for Effective Christian Leadership.* Grand Rapids, MI: Baker Academic, 2008.

Litfin, Duane. *Conceiving the Christian College: A College President Shares His Vision of Christian Higher Education.* Grand Rapids, MI: Wm. B. Eerdmans, 2004.

Livermore, David. *Driven by Difference: How Great Companies Fuel Innovation through Diversity.* New York: American Management Association, 2016.

Longman, Karen A. and Patricia S. Anderson. "Women in Leadership: The Future of Christian Higher Education," *Christian Higher Education* 15:1–2 (2016) 24–37.

Longman, Karen. *Diversity Matters: Race, Ethnicity, and the Future of Christian Higher Education.* Abilene Christian University Press, 2017.

Lopez, Gloria. "Pa'Lante! Toward the Presidency: Understanding Factors that Facilitate Latino Leadership in Higher Education." EdD diss., University of Massachusetts, 2014.

Lumina Foundation. "A Stronger Nation through Higher Education." Indianapolis: Lumina Foundation, 2015. http://www.luminafoundation.org/files/publications/A _stronger_nation_through_higher_education- 2015.pdf.

Malavé, I., and E. Giordani. *Latino Stats: American Hispanics by the Numbers.* New York: The New Press, 2015.

Martinez, A. E. "U.S. Hispanic/Latino biblical interpretation: A critique from within." *Theology Today* 68:2 (2011) 134–148.

Martínez, F. Juan. *Los Protestantes: An Introduction to Latino Protestantism in the United States.* Santa Barbara, CA: Praeger, 2011.

———. *The Story of Latino Protestants in the United States.* Grand Rapids, MI: Wm. B. Eerdmans, 2018.

———. *Walk with the People: Latino Ministry in the United States.* Nashville, TN: Abingdon Press, 2008.

McConnell, Douglas. *Cultural Insights for Christian Leaders: New Directions for Organizations Serving God's Mission.* Mission in Global Community. Grand Rapids, MI: Baker Academic, 2018.

Mendenhall, Mark E., et al. *Global Leadership: Research, Practice, and Development.* New York: Routledge Taylor & Francis, 2018.

Moffitt, Michael J. "A Narrative Study of the Experiences of Executive Administrators of Color Who Work at Religiously-Affiliated Higher Education Institutions." EdD/HE diss., Azuza Pacific University, 2017.

Moreau, A. Scott. *Contextualization in World Missions: Mapping and Assessing Evangelical Models.* Grand Rapids, MI: Kregel, 2012.

Motel, Seth and Eileen Patten. Pew Research Center, "Hispanic Origin Profiles, 2010." *Pew Research Center,* 2012. http://www.pewhispanic.org/2012/06/27/country-of-origin-profiles/.

NAACP. "Criminal Justice Fact Sheet." https://naacp.org/resources/criminal-justice-fact-sheet.

Nkomo, Stella M. Akram Al Ariss. "The Historical Origins of Ethnic (White) Privilege in US Organizations." *Journal of Managerial Psychology* 29, 4 (2014) 389.

Northouse, G. Peter. *Leadership: Theory and Practice,* 7th ed. Thousand Oaks, CA: SAGE Publications, 2016.

Núñez, Anne-Marie, et al. "Latinos in Higher Education and Hispanic-Serving Institutions: Creating Conditions for Success." *ASHE Higher Education Report* 39:1. Hoboken, NJ: Wiley/Jossey-Bass, 2013.

Núñez, Anne-Marie, et al. *Hispanic-Serving Institutions: Advancing Research and Transformative Practice.* New York: Routledge, 2015.

Nussbaum, Kathleen B., and Heewon Chang. "The Quest for Diversity in Christian Higher Education: Building Institutional Governance Capacity." *Christian Higher Education* 12:1–2 (2013) 5–19.

Obenchain, Alice M., et al. 2010. "Institutional Types, Organizational Cultures, and Innovation in Christian Colleges and Universities." *Christian Higher Education* 3:1 (2010) 15–39.

Ortiz, Paul. *An African American and Latinx History of the United States.* Boston, MA: Beacon, 2018.

Paredes-Collins, Kristin. "Cultivating Diversity and Spirituality: A Compelling Interest for Institutional Priority." *Christian Higher Education* 12:1–2 (2013) 122–37.

Patterson, James A. *Shining Lights: A History of the Council for Christian Colleges & Universities.* Grand Rapids, MI.: Baker Academic, 2001.

Pérez, Joel. "Diversity at Christian Colleges: It's about Mission." *Christian Higher Education* 12:1–2 (2013) 20–34.

Peterson, Brooks. *Cultural Intelligence: A Guide to Working with People from Other Cultures.* Boston: Intercultural, 2004.

Poe, Harry Lee. *Christianity in the Academy: Teaching at the Intersection of Faith and Learning.* Grand Rapids, MI: Baker Academic, 2004.

Prentiss, Craig R., ed. *Religion and the Creation of Race and Ethnicity: An Introduction.* New York: New York University Press, 2003.

Pulpit & Pen. "4 Main Things Christians Need to Know About Critical Race Theory." October 20, 2020. https://pulpitandpen.org/2019/08/06/4-main-things-christians-need-to-know-about-critical-race-theory/

Ragone, Nick. *The Everything American Government Book: From Constitution to Present-day Elections, All You Need to Understand Our Democratic System.* Avon, MA: Simon & Schuster, 2004.

Rah, Soong-Chan. *The Next Evangelicalism: Releasing the Church from Western Cultural Captivity.* Downers Grove, IL: InterVarsity, 2009.

Ramírez-Johnson, Johnny and Edwin L. Hernandez. *Avance: A Vision for a New Mañana.* Loma Linda, CA: Loma Linda University Press, 2003.

Regent University, School of Business and Leadership, Commissioning Service 2021. https://www.regent.edu/admin/media/live_commissioning/?live_event_name=sbl.

Ringenberg, William C, and Mark A. Noll. *The Christian College: A History of Protestant Higher Education in America.* 2nd ed. Grand Rapids, MI: Baker Academic, 2006.

Robinson, Elaine A. *Race and Theology. Horizons in Theology.* Nashville, TN: Abingdon, 2012.

Rodríguez, Cristóbal, et al. "Latino Educational Leadership Across the Pipeline." *Journal of Hispanic Higher Education* 15:2 (2016) 136–53.

Rodríguez, Jose, and Loida Martell-Ortero. *Teologia En Conjunto: A Collaborative Hispanic Protestant Theology.* Louisville, KY: Westminster John Knox, 1997.

Rodríguez, Rubén Rosario. *Racism and God-Talk: A Latino/a Perspective.* New York: New York University Press, 2008.

Romero, Robert Chao. *Brown Church: Five Centuries of Latina/o Social Justice, Theology, and Identity.* Downers Grove, IL: InterVarsity, 2020.

Roxburgh, Alan J., and Fred Romanuk. *The Missional Leader: Equipping Your Church to Reach a Changing World.* Leadership Network Publication. San Francisco, CA: Jossey-Bass, 2006.

Salinas, Cristobal Jr. and Adele Lozano. "Mapping and Recontextualizing the Evolution of the Term Latinx: An Environmental Scanning in Higher Education." *Journal of Latinos and Education* 18:4 (2017) 302–315.

Salinas, Cristobal, Jr. "Transforming Academia and Theorizing Spaces for Latinx in Higher Education: "Voces Perdidas" and "Voces De Poder."" *International Journal of Qualitative Studies in Education* 30:8 (2017) 746–58.

Sanchez, D. R. *Hispanic Realities Impacting America: Implications for Evangelism and Missions.* Fort Worth, TX: Church Starting Network, 2006.

Santiago, Deborah A., and Patrick Callan. "Ensuring America's Future: Benchmarking Latino College Completion to Meet National Goals: 2010 to 2020." 2010. Washington, D.C.: Excelencia in Education, 2010.

Santiago, Deborah A., and Megan Soliz. "Ensuring America's Future by Increasing Latino College Completion: Latino College Completion in 50 States." 2012. Washington, D.C.: Excelencia in Education, 2012.

Savala, Leonard A. III. 2014. "The Experiences of Latina/o Executives in Higher Education." PhD diss., Western Michigan University, 2014.

Sechrest, Love L., et al, eds. *Can "White" People Be Saved? Triangulating Race, Theology, and Mission.* Downers Grove, IL: InterVarsity, 2018.

Schein, Peter H. and Edgar A. Schein. *Organizational Culture and Leadership.* 5th ed. Hoboken, NJ: John Wiley and Sons, 2017.

Shenvi, Neil. "Critical Race Theory and Christianity." *Christian Apologetics from a Homeschooling Theoretical Chemist.* October 20, 2020. https://shenviapologetics.com/critical-race-theory-and-christianity/.

Sherman, Christopher, et al. "US Held Record Number of Migrant Children in Custody in 2019." Associated Press. November 12, 2019.

Sherwood, Harriet. "White Evangelical Christians Stick by Trump Again, Exit Polls Show." https://www.theguardian.com/us-news/2020/nov/06/white-evangelical-christians-supported-trump.

Smith, G. Daryl. *Diversity's Promise for Higher Education: Making it Work.* Baltimore, MD: John Hopkins University Press, 2015.

Solorzano, D. and Tara J. Yosso. "Critical Race and LatCrit Theory and Method: Counter-storytelling," *International Journal of Qualitative Studies in Education* 14:4 (2010) 471–495.

Solorzano, D., and Tara Yosso. "Critical Race Methodology: Counter Storytelling as an Analytical Framework." *Qualitative Inquiry* 8:1 (2002) 23–44.

Souto-Manning, Mariana. 2014. "Critical Narrative Analysis: The Interplay of Critical Discourse and Narrative Analyses." *International Journal of Qualitative Studies in Education* 27:2 (2014) 159–180.

Thelin, John R. *A History of American Higher Education,* 2nd ed. Baltimore, MD: Johns Hopkins University Press, 2011.

Ting-Toomey, Stella, and Leeva C. Chung. *Understanding Intercultural Communication.* Los Angeles: Roxbury, 2004.

Tucker, Ruth. *From Jerusalem to Irian Jaya: A Biographical History of Christian Missions.* 2nd ed. Grand Rapids, MI: Zondervan, 2004.

United States Census Bureau. 2017. "Quick Facts United States." https://www.census.gov/quickfacts/fact/table/US/PST045217.

———. "U.S. Census Bureau Releases New Educational Attainment Data." 2020. https://www.census.gov/newsroom/press-releases/2020/educational-attainment.html

Valdes, Francisco. "Foreword: Under Construction—LatCrit Consciousness, Community, and Theory." *California Law Review* 85:5 (1997) 1087–1142.

Van Velso, E., et al. *The Center for Creative Leadership Handbook of Leadership Development.* 3rd ed. San Francisco, CA: Jossey-Bass, 2010.

Villalpando, Octavio. "Practical Considerations of Critical Race Theory and Latino Critical Theory for Latino College Students." *New Directions for Student Services* 105 (2004) 41–50.

Villarruel, A. "A Framework for Latino Nursing Leadership." *Nursing Science Quarterly* 30:4 (2017) 347–352.

Wildavsky, Ben, et al, eds. *Reinventing Higher Education: The Promise of Innovation.* Cambridge, MA: Harvard Education Press, 2012.

Williams, Damon A. *Strategic Diversity Leadership: Activating Change and Transformation in Higher Education.* Sterling, VA: Stylus, 2013.

Williams, Damon A., and Katrina C. Wade-Golden. *The Chief Diversity Officer: Strategy, Structure, and Change Management.* 1st ed. Sterling, VA: Stylus, 2013.

Wise, Tim. "Is Sisterhood Conditional? White Women and the Rollback of Affirmative Action." *NWSA Journal* 10:3 (1998) 126.

Yancey, George A. *Neither Jew nor Gentile: Exploring Issues of Racial Diversity on Protestant College Campuses.* New York: Oxford University Press, 2010.

Yosso, T.J. 2005. *Critical Race Counterstories Along the Chicana/o Educational Pipeline.* New York: Routledge, 2006.

———. "Whose Culture has Capital? A Critical Race Theory Discussion of Community Cultural Wealth." *Race Ethnicity and Education* 8:1 (2005) 69–91.

Yukl, Gary A. *Leadership in Organizations.* Boston: Pearson, 2013.

CPSIA information can be obtained
at www.ICGtesting.com
Printed in the USA
BVHW061221300122
627305BV00005B/16